PROBATION VALUES

Brian Williams (editor)

VENTURE PRESS

Published by
VENTURE PRESS
16 Kent Street
Birmingham
B5 6RD
Tel: 0121 622 3911

First published 1995

British Library Cataloguing-in-Publication Data.
A catalogue record for this book is available from the British Library.

ISBN 187 3878 125 (paperback)

Printed and bound in Great Britain by
Biddles Ltd, Guildford and King's Lynn

Contents

(i)

Acknowledgments

This book took a long time to plan and write, and I am grateful to those who helped me to develop the original idea, particularly Robert Adams, Sally Arkley and Jane Watt. During the writing and editing of the book, several people gave generously of their time, and while they are not to blame for any errors, they have helped to eliminate some. Caterina Fagg, Mike Nellis and Sue Roberts gave particularly valuable help, although they may not have known it at the time.

The other contributors, of course, helped me to sort out my ideas and collaborated effectively with each other. I especially want to thank Bryan Gocke for stepping in at short notice when another contributor was unable to continue due to illness: his chapter shows no signs of the pressure under which it was prepared. Anne Worrall took her responsibility seriously, and her thoughtful and balanced comments on other chapters were most welcome.

Finally, I want to acknowledge the influence and help of my students and colleagues at Keele, Sheffield and Teesside, and of probation colleagues and clients in Staffordshire, South Yorkshire, Warwickshire and Durham over the years.

Brian Williams
Keele, October 1994

About the contributors

Jon Arnold is a Lecturer in Social Work at Exeter University. His main areas of interest include the teaching of Applied Criminology, Counselling, and Probation and Social Work Practice. He is currently assisting with the design and creation of a maritime alternative to youth custody project.

Bill Beaumont lectures in Social Work at Bristol University, with a special focus on probation training. He was a probation officer in Inner London for 15 years and General Secretary of NAPO from 1985-92. His publications include two books - Probation Work (1981) written jointly with Hilary Walker, and Working with Offenders, edited with Hilary Walker. Current research and writing interests include user research and empowerment practice in the probation setting.

Anne Celnick is Research Officer for South Yorkshire Probation Service and research advisor to the Association of Chief Officers of Probation. She has written about the place of social work help in probation practice, experimental projects and the relationship between race and rehabilitation. Her current research interests include the development of practice evaluation and the attitudes of criminal justice practitioners to the criminal justice system.

Bryan Gocke is a probation officer who specialises in working with perpetrators of sexual offences, and a freelance trainer and consultant in this area of work. He has previously written about the effect processing through the criminal justice system has on sex offenders' denial (Tackling Denial in Sex Offenders, a Probation Monograph published by the University of East Anglia in 1991). He is an active member of the National Association for the Development of Work with Sex Offenders.

Bill Jordan worked in an English probation service from 1965 to 1974, and has taught social work, social policy and politics at Exeter and Huddersfield Universities, and in Germany, the Netherlands and Denmark. He has researched and published widely on social justice, social work and social policy.

Bill McWilliams joined the Probation Service in 1962. He worked as a probation officer, senior probation officer and, for ten years, as Research Officer for the South Yorkshire Probation Service. For four years he was a member of the Home Office Research Unit, where he worked on the National Probation Project. Currently he is a senior member of Wolfson College, Cambridge and a visiting scholar at the Institute of Criminology, Cambridge. He has published widely on probation related matters.

(iii)

Una Padel is the Co-ordinator of London Prisons Community Links. She worked as a probation officer from 1981 to 1985, and was Deputy Director of the Prison Reform Trust from 1985 to 1989. From 1989 to 1993 she was an Assistant Director at the Standing Conference on Drug Abuse, where she managed projects designed to provide better information about HIV and AIDS to prisoners and people living in probation hostels, and to improve the way in which the criminal justice system deals with drug users. She is co-author, with Prue Stevenson, of Insiders: women's experience of prison (Virago, 1988) and, with Rose Twidale and John Porter, of HIV education in prisons: a resource book (Health Education Authority, 1992).

Andrew Shephard, a former probation officer, works in a voluntary sector organisation providing services for people with alcohol and drug problems. He is author of Substance Dependency, published by Venture Press in 1990, and is a regular contributor to social work magazines. He is currently studying the interaction of technology and social care.

Brian Williams is a lecturer in the Department of Applied Social Studies at the University of Keele. He has researched and written on a wide range of criminal justice issues, and worked as a probation officer for most of the period from 1981 to 1993, gradually moving into full-time education and training. He has been active in opposing the deprofessionalisation of probation training.

Anne Worrall has been a lecturer in Criminology at Keele University since 1993. Prior to that, she was Director of the MA/Diploma programme at Keele and had responsibility for probation training. She has worked as a Social Work Lecturer at Manchester University and as a probation officer in Staffordshire. She has researched and published in the area of women and crime, as author of Offending Women, published by Routledge in 1990 and co-editor (with Pat Carlen) of Gender, Crime and Justice published by the Open University Press in 1987. She has also researched the changing role of prison Boards of Visitors and is author of Have you got a minute?, published by the Prison Reform Trust in 1994.

ONE: INTRODUCTION
Brian Williams

The authors of this book argue that values must underpin professional practice, and that social work values are, and must remain, the foundation of probation work. The connection between probation and social work values is under attack, and this Introduction will examine some of the reasons for this. It will then go on to attempt to define the main values underlying professional probation practice, without repeating too much of the material already available elsewhere. Some of the contradictions and difficulties which arise when trying to put these values into practice will be briefly examined. Finally, the ensuing chapters will be outlined for the reader who wishes to use the book selectively.

First, a few words about the process by which the book came into existence. The contributors include practitioners, academics and managers who all have a probation background. They have collaborated in writing their chapters, and if my own experience was anything to go by, their contributions have been greatly improved by discussing drafts with the other authors as the book progressed. No uniform definitions were imposed on the writers, and indeed this Introduction was almost the last chapter to be written. This was deliberate: the authors cover a range of ideological positions and come from diverse backgrounds, with only their probation expertise in common, and it seemed best to let them define the issues for themselves, within a broad outline of the area to be covered and the thrust of the book. Although at times nerve-racking for an editor, the results do seem to have justified this strategy. Differing perspectives have been applied to a number of practice issues and areas in a very productive way.

The main purpose of the book is to provide an opportunity to raise the level of debate about probation values. Left to CCETSW and the Home Office, the value base could easily be subsumed by tick-lists of competences (which would, of course, refer to the need for the profession to be founded on certain key values, without specifying on any but the most superficial level what these might be). Some of those involved in social work education, including some of the contributors to the present volume, have begun to specify what we would substitute for the tick-lists (Jones, 1993; Nellis, forthcoming; Jordan, 1993; Divine, 1991; Ahmed, 1991).

WHY SOCIAL WORK VALUES UNDERPIN PROBATION PRACTICE - AND WHY THE CONNECTION IS UNDER ATTACK

Probation officers, probation trainers and members of related interest groups like NAPO tend to speak of probation values as if it were obvious what these are. The nature of the value base on which probation work rests seems almost to be defined by the threats it faces. Only when a new proposal or development is opposed do we tend to invoke probation values as an argument against it. This has been the case, over the years, as the functions of the probation service have changed.

When parole was introduced, it was vehemently opposed on the grounds that it would involve "a new authoritarianism". (Monger, 1972,10) In practice, however, probation officers avoided this by treating most parolees in much the same way as they had always treated probationers (Monger, 1972; Morris & Beverly, 1975). At the time of the passage of the relevant legislation, NAPO's main concern was to ensure that sufficient resources were made available for the work to be done properly, although reservations were also expressed about the probation officer's role in recalling clients who did not comply with the conditions of parole (Bochel, 1976).

Similarly, many probation staff reacted adversely to the proposed introduction of Community Service Orders (Walker & Beaumont, 1981), arguing that enforcing such orders, which had no social work content, made probation officers into "screws on wheels" as well as spreading the carceral net more widely. The introduction of such work, explicitly involving punishment of offenders, was widely seen as incompatible with the values of the service (Varah, 1987). In this case, however, the measure was so popular with the public and the politicians that NAPO again confined itself to arguing for additional resources to implement the new measure, and it was introduced gradually.

More recently, the combination order and electronic tagging have aroused similar feelings - and more concerted and principled opposition from both NAPO and the penal reform lobby. The introduction of national standards - first in relation to community service and later regulating all areas of probation work - gave the government much greater power over the nature of probation officers' contact with clients. The 1991 Criminal Justice Act, while in many ways a progressive development, made it clear that the probation order itself was to be seen as a punishment, and most of the forward-looking, anti-custodial aspects of the legislation were repealed by the 1993 Act only months after they came into force. Each step towards a more controlling probation service has been greeted by statements of the need to defend probation values against such changes. In the period since 1988, however, the government has been increasingly hostile to such arguments. Rapid change has moved the service substantially towards "community corrections" and the government's commitment to punishment in the community is reminiscent of Foucault's "disciplinary society".

To some extent, the appeal to probation values was effective in influencing the course of developments until the late 1980s. NAPO opposed curfews as part of supervision orders in 1988 and again in 1991, and although the Criminal Justice Acts contained provision for such curfews, professional opposition was recognised by sentencers and few such orders were made. The opposition focused on the need to defend the values of clients' dignity and right to self-determination. The proposals of the Younger Report in the 1970s were also effectively opposed: probation officers made it clear through NAPO that they did not welcome the possibility of being given the power to have clients held in custody overnight for failing to comply with instructions, and that they would be reluctant to exercise such powers. Again, opposition was rooted in basic social work values: anti-custodialism and a preference for positive relationships with clients rather than crude disciplinary powers.

The unions and the penal reform lobby have had to change their tactics in the face of Government intransigence over professional issues since the late 1980s. NAPO and the Association of Black Probation Officers, for example, became heavily involved in the process of drafting the 1992 national standards and the 1994 competences. Only by doing so were they allowed to influence the contents. The price of such involvement is that the scope for effective opposition to the policies enshrined in the documents after their publication is necessarily reduced, but the final product reflects implicit service values far more than it would have done if the job had been left to the Civil Service. In the case of the national standards, the rigidity of the draft requirements on breaching clients who did not comply with conditions of supervision was greatly reduced: self-determination and anti-custodial values were at least partially upheld. The competences for main grade probation officers were repeatedly amended to include anti-oppressive practice requirements and to omit mechanistic references to enforcement.

The influence of the unions and campaigning groups has declined considerably, but they remain prepared to stand up for the social work values of the probation service in extreme cases. The voluntary

3

sector has a creditable record of opposition to youth prisons on social work grounds (see for example NAJC, 1994), and of demanding the implementation of section 95 of the 1991 Act and calling on the Government to match its equal opportunities rhetoric with appropriate action (NACRO, 1992). NAPO has also been active in these areas, and has been prepared to support industrial action in defence of clients' rights (for example, in instructing members not to prepare court reports on defendants who were pleading not guilty).

Government opposition to the principles on which the probation service bases its work has become increasingly strident. Anti-custo-dialism has been attacked by politicians, including the Prime Minister, despite the government's apparent conversion to the cause under previous leadership. According to the 1990 Green Paper, prison is "an expensive way of making bad people worse". Only three years later, the next Home Secretary declared, with the Prime Minister's backing, that "prison works". The very connection between social work and probation has come under ideological assault, with a minister going so far as to suggest that ex-soldiers would be more appropriate probation officers than the existing, social-work-trained staff (Travis, 1994). This was not a new or isolated denial of the necessity of a connection between social work and probation: from the early 1980s, the basis of probation training occurring on social work qualifying courses was repeatedly ques-tioned (for example in the 1990 Green Paper (Home Office, 1990); see also Nellis, forthcoming), and formally reviewed.

The connection between social work and probation values therefore needs justification. The obvious reason for the link is historical: the probation service grew up alongside the social work profession and shares its basic principles. This, of course, is not a sufficient reason for it to continue to espouse social work values: other professions have broken away from the principles which governed the activities of their originators, as in the case of Borstal assistant governors, who began by seeing themselves as closely linked to social workers but whose successors are now clear about their identity as prison governors.

Nevertheless, the historical links are strong. As the Christian values of British social workers came under question, secular varia-tions evolved, and although the probation service distanced itself from the unitary social work departments in England and Wales, Scottish social work retained its involvement with adult offenders including probationers and prisoners. Removing probation workers from generic training courses in England and Wales would not quickly demolish the common value base: generic work would presumably continue north of the border, and it would take forty years for all the social-work-trained staff in the probation service to retire.

The attack on the genericism of social work training has always had an ideological undertow. Although some academics, employers and practitioners find the balance between social work and probation teaching to be in need of adjustment, the overwhelming majority defend generic training on principle. It is distasteful to Conservative ministers for precisely the same reasons: generic training upholds social work values and acts as a corrective against the more punitive extremes of the "just deserts" philosophy. Those who wish to placate the Conservatives speak and write of the probation service as a "corrections" rather than a social work service, and in doing so they explicitly reject social work values[1].

Other arguments for the social work/probation link are more compelling. Probation officers and social workers have similar powers and deal with clients who have broadly similar problems - indeed in many cases their clients are the same people. Despite their separate administrative structures and increasingly diverging functions, probation officers and social workers see themselves as part of the same profession, and they liaise with the same range of other professions. Like social work, probation is "a moral activity which requires practitioners and managers to make decisions which are primarily concerned with the restriction of a person's liberty" (Ward & Spencer, 1994, 97), and this means there is a need for agreed and enforceable ethical standards.

Whatever politicians may say, there is a clear consensus that probation is part of social work, and this is primarily because of their largely shared value base. There are, however, one or two dissenting voices. Mike Nellis, for example, has been energetic and persuasive in arguing that probation officers should no longer be trained as social workers and that the value base of probation work is ill-served by CCETSW's fumbling attempts to articulate it (Nellis, 1993 and forthcoming). He suggests that criminology offers a more appropriate discipline than social work for the training of probation officers, although there is of course no such thing as a criminologist in practice with clients.

Much of the literature about social work values was published in the 1970s, when there was more of a consensus about the purpose of social work than there has been in the subsequent period. For example, a working party convened by CCETSW claimed in 1976 that although social work might be seen as an agent of social control, it exercised this function in a "humane rather than punitive" way (CCETSW, 1976, 40)[2]. This statement was questionable at the time, but seems more contentious now than perhaps it was then. Two decades of political and social polarisation make it seem naïve and even disingenuous. But it is revealing, too. Such a bland summary of the care versus control debate was possible in the 1970s. Now, when it is a constant struggle to justify the need for services to be delivered in sensitive, caring and responsive ways, it is more difficult to pretend that probation work is at the controlling end of the social work continuum, and generic social work primarily concerned with delivering care. Control is no longer simply a function of the association of some parts of social work with the criminal courts: it is an explicit function of many other services in which it was formerly implicit or altogether hidden. Paradoxically, this makes it clearer than ever that probation work draws its values from social work.

The social work profession has been forced to accept that one of its major functions is the control of a threatening underclass, and while the probation service has an important part to play in this (Simon, 1993; Drakeford, 1993), so do social workers in other areas such as youth justice (Children's Society, 1993; Goldson, 1994), mental health and community care (Biggs, 1990; Drakeford, 1993a) and so on. The CCETSW working party acknowledged that social workers' powers, like those of probation officers, are defined by law, but made much of the professional authority involved in working with voluntary clients (a very much larger group in the 1970s than in the 1990s, of course). It discussed the proposals of the Younger Report (see above) in terms of a danger of shifting probation work towards "exercising control on behalf of the courts". Few probation officers or social workers can today be in any doubt that this is one of their central functions.

Historically, the probation service has been a branch of social work which has never been able to deny its intimate involvement in enforcing court orders. Since the 1960s, many probation officers have believed that they as professionals should determine the nature of their intervention with clients, and that crude control is unlikely to be the most effective way of encouraging individual change, but they have not sought to avoid the fact that the courts are the source of their powers. The debate on the Younger Report was revealing in that it highlighted these claims to professionalism as social workers and to expertise in helping relationships which did not depend mainly upon coercion (Holden, 1974 and London Branch of NAPO, 1975, both quoted in Walker & Beaumont, 1981, 93-5). The same claims have been made in response to the other threats to probation

6

officers' social work values given as examples above: the introduction of parole was opposed on the grounds that it involved unhelpful and unnecessary limitations on clients' self-determination and, as such, it fettered probation officers' professional discretion. So also with electronic tagging. Community service removed the helping relationship from client supervision, reducing it to mere supervision, which does not require professional expertise - and as such, community service work has been largely hived off to unqualified staff.

In this sense, probation staff have relied upon social work values in making decisions about what forms of control they are prepared to exercise. Their proximity to the courts, and then to the parole board and increasingly to the prison service, has forced them to maintain an awareness of ethical constraints and issues. They have constantly had to maintain a "balancing act between social work and criminal justice" (Parsloe, 1991, 53). As the rest of the social work profession has been forced into a more controlling role, the experience of the probation service has to some extent been drawn upon (for example, after the pin-down scandal, in determining what kinds of restraint are acceptable in controlling young offenders). The traffic has been two-way, and indeed the probation service has arguably learnt more from its membership of the social work profession than vice versa. The obvious example is the influence of systems management and the doctrine of minimum intervention upon probation work with young offenders in the period from the mid-1970s to the passage of the 1991 Criminal Justice Act.

It seems, then, that for historical and political reasons it is inevitable that the probation service will continue to appeal to its basis in social work values when attempting to see the moral way ahead. Had different decisions been made at crucial points in history, this might not now be the case:

for example, it would have been possible at the time of local government reorganisation in the 1970s for the probation service to ally itself more closely with the police or prison service, or indeed with the medical profession. In the event, the continuing association with social work has dictated the nature of the response to significant threats, and it has also determined the type of training probation officers receive.

While the value base might remain implicit in such training, it is very clearly a social work base.

From this base probation work has to some extent gone on in its own distinct direction. Work with offenders is not exclusive to social workers who specialise in probation work, and nor do they

7

only work with offenders, but the offender focus of the work has led to some traditional social work values being comparatively under-emphasised in probation work. On the other hand, the probation service has developed some aspects of the value base for its own use in distinctive ways.

In 1990, when it formulated the rules ("Paper 30") by which DipSW programmes of qualifying training for social workers would be validated, CCETSW produced a brief list of "the values of social work", slightly amplified in respect of probation training the following year (CCETSW, 1991). The former differed little from those generated by the 1976 working party, but the latter, probation-specific statement emphasised "the potential for conflict between organizational, professional and individual values", the need for what CCETSW was still at that time calling "anti-oppressive" practice[3], and the capacity to manage tensions between different actors in the criminal justice system.

As noted above, CCETSW commissioned a firm of consultants to re-work the competences in Paper 30 in 1994. As part of this process, a list of the values underlying social work was generated. These were much blander and less comprehensive than those in the 1976 and 1991 documents, which is why this discussion has concentrated upon the former.

The treatment of all clients as unique individuals has, in my view, been regrettably under-emphasised in recent probation practice. The criminal justice system both individualises social problems and depersonalises the processing of individual offenders (Williams, 1993). The probation service has too often been part of the problem in the depersonalising to which imprisoned offenders are subjected (Williams, 1992), a situation which is discussed further in the chapter on throughcare in this book. It may be that respect for clients as individuals has suffered from changing social policies affecting all areas of social work, but it is very noticeable in probation work. The positive meaning of individualisation - the exploration of a client's concerns in an atmosphere of affirmation of his or her individuality - and its negative meaning - the blaming of the individual for social ills - are not always clearly distinguished.

Generations of workers have been socialised into bureaucratic practices, and in the process the benefits of individualised working can get lost (Rojek *et al.*, 1988).

Changing management theories and practices have also played a part in reducing the emphasis on this vital ethical principle of social work, in probation (McWilliams, 1992; Thomas & Vanstone, 1992) and elsewhere (Lipsky, 1978; Hardy, 1981; Hale, 1983). As feminist writers have pointed out, managerialism converts moral issues into technical ones, political questions into administrative ones (Hardy, 1981). Social work cannot afford continually to commit resources to bureaucratic management at the expense of individual work with clients, because "in the long term that a profession should devalue the performance of its primary task can only be to its detriment" (Hale, 1983, 185). There is a real danger that management is seen as somehow value-free, and its success therefore actually becomes "related to its ability to simplify value-structures" (Christie, 1993, 167).

Other aspects of social work values are particularly emphasised and highly-developed in contemporary probation practice. Some of these have also been developed in other ways by different kinds of social workers. For example, concern for victims and potential victims of crime is crucial to probation work and to child protection work, as is a separation of some kind between the work with offenders or perpetrators and that with victims.

The need for such a separation presents social workers with something of a dilemma: how is it to be achieved, without disadvantage to either the offender or the victimised? Social work often throws up such dilemmas, and they can to some extent be solved by simply allocating different workers to undertake potentially conflicting parts of a task; one social worker might deal with the perpetrator and his offending behaviour while another facilitates the victim's recovery. It can sometimes be important for an individual worker to effect some similar kind of separation: for example, between the offender as a valued human being and as an offender. This, too, is familiar to those in various specialist areas of social work practice: probation officers work with individuals and groups of offenders looking at and sometimes challenging in quite forceful ways their offending behaviour, but the same probation officer will also be involved in providing individual supervision and help to the clients. Similar issues concerning the "ethics of influence" (Jordan, 1993) affect social workers who are responsible for teaching clients with learning difficulties how to behave in socially acceptable ways in public, and education social workers dealing with school refusal.

While not unique to probation practice, there are also some principles which are particularly highly developed by those working with offenders. An obvious example is opposition to custody (although of course youth justice social workers have pioneered much of the good practice in this area, and the whole community care movement began with challenges to the efficacy of institutionalisation by social workers, educationists, criminologists and sociologists in the

1960s). It is, and must be, basic to the professionalism and claim to moral authority of the probation service that it opposes the use of custody - although the social work training council has been strangely silent about this in its pronouncements on professional values (Nellis, 1993). By bringing to bear their knowledge and experience of the damage caused by imprisonment, probation officers are in a unique position to influence the courts to limit such outcomes, and to inform the development of penal policy if and when politicians show any inclination to listen.

The penal system also gives rise to another area of professional values where the probation service has to some extent gone its own way, although again, developments in probation have been paralleled elsewhere. In the area of confidentiality, the probation interface with prisons has both constrained and encouraged change. Probation officers have insisted upon a degree of openness with their clients which has until recently been uncongenial and threatening to prison staff. The Woolf report gave tentative developments in information sharing pioneered by probation officers a healthy push, as did a number of European court cases initiated by UK prisoners, and the prison system is now slowly moving towards greater openness in a number of areas: sentence planning involves individual prisoners, reasons have to be given for parole decisions, lifers' tariff date has to be made known, written reports can be seen by clients. While other agencies led the way in instituting client access to social work files (Payne, 1989), the probation service implemented its values by working towards and implementing these other changes - although the system, including the probation service, still makes the decisions about which information to share, and to this extent the changes can be seen as cosmetic and paternalistic (Sainsbury, 1989).

Similarly, probation officers have interpreted the need to deal with injustice rather differently from colleagues in other areas of social work. This area is still underdeveloped, and at times those in Social Services Departments and voluntary agencies seem to have been at the forefront of progressive practice. It was youth justice workers, for example, who pioneered an appeals strategy which means that young offenders - and particularly young women and young black people - should always be given appropriate assistance if sentenced oppressively in the youth court (Pitts, 1988; Nellis, 1991; Rutherford, 1992). But probation teams have given high priority to anti-discriminatory practice in the writing and monitoring of court reports (Kett *et al.*, 1992), and to devising strategies for the effective supervision of racially-motivated offenders. While probation officers have individually often been circumspect about lending the service's name to attacks on racial injustice, a good deal of work has been done by the service to highlight the racialised nature of policing and court practices (Kett *et al.*, 1992; see also CADP, 1992).

WHAT THE VALUES UNDERLYING PROBATION WORK ARE

There is no agreed list of probation values, and such a list would probably not be particularly helpful: mechanical references to "confidentiality", for example, can be a way of avoiding discussion of complex ethical issues (Shardlow, 1991; Timms, 1983; Rojek *et al.*, 1988). But several writers have produced similar sets of basic principles, derived from social work values, which they see as underlying probation practice. It is important to note that there is no "official" value base, perhaps because NAPO, unlike BASW, has chosen to leave the matter open. (NAPO is opposed to the formation of a General Social Work Council whose members would be required to confirm their agreement to a documented code of ethics, while BASW supports the development of a professional body of this kind and has devised a code of ethics (BASW, 1975). The arguments for and against the GSWC are not relevant to the present discussion). Any such "official" formulation must, by its nature, be regarded with suspicion, and so must what follows! A committee or an individual is free to try to formulate the value base underlying a profession, but must take the consequences if it does not accurately reflect the views of others committed to the profession.

The work of Bryan Williams and of Phyllida Parsloe is particularly helpful in defining the key values of the probation service, and both have been drawn upon in writing the next section. Bill Jordan's thoughts on the teaching of values to DipSW students are also extremely thought-provoking, as are Mike Nellis's writings on probation training (Williams, 1993; Parsloe, 1991; Jordan, 1993; Nellis, 1993). What follows, however, has to be regarded as part of a continuing discussion. It is presented in that spirit, and not as a definitive list of the values of the probation community.

* OPPOSITION TO CUSTODY

An anti-custodial stance, it seems to me, is a fundamental value underlying probation work. From the earliest days of probation work, when police court missionaries were primarily concerned with offenders' moral reform and rescue, they worked with people who had been refused the assistance of others, including prisoners. This arose partly from respect for individuals, motivated by Christian belief in the inherent worth of all human beings, but it led logically to an opposition to the use of custody. The court missionaries were motivated partly by the prospect of keeping individual offenders out of prison, and their records show that they achieved this in large numbers of cases. Many probation officers were subsequently active in Quaker and other religious groups involved in penal reform, and later in secular campaigning organisations opposing custody and advocating better prison conditions.

Recourse to prison was common for minor offences in the late nineteenth and early twentieth centuries, and the early probation service concentrated its efforts on women and young offenders, who were thought most likely to be susceptible to reform. With the increasing use of pre-sentence reports and statutory supervision after release from prison, probation officers came into more and more contact with the prisons. Opposition to custody became increasingly central to the value base.

The corollary of this was increasing involvement in the provision of non-custodial sentences. Again, this goes back a long way. When a police court missionary offered to supervise an offender in the community, this paved the way for the probation order. As new opportunities to provide non-custodial measures arose, the probation service was centrally involved - although concern for clients' rights and dignity often meant that such involvement was cautious. The underlying principle of minimum intervention (which has remained an important influence in many fields of social work) goes back to Bentham's notion of frugality: he argued that punishment was an evil to be avoided wherever possible and carefully rationed (Bentham, 1970, 179-80).

The underlying concern has been to deal with offenders in constructive ways which do not degrade or damage them. This is related to the other values of client self-determination and potential for change, but it is so central for probation workers that it deserves to be seen as a distinctive principle:

* Probation workers are opposed to the use of custodial punishments and committed to the use and provision of more constructive ways of dealing with offenders.

* OPPOSITION TO OPPRESSION AND COMMITMENT TO JUSTICE FOR OFFENDERS

Probation workers have only recently begun to see the need for anti-oppressive practice, and the profession of social work does not have a creditable history in this respect. Probation practice has reinforced the stereotyping and labelling of offenders, and not all within the profession subscribe to the values of anti-oppressive practice (see for example Pinker, 1993).

Of all the values on which modern probation practice is based, this is therefore the most fragile and contested. That it is contested is no bad thing in some respects: the social work training council has helped to create a rather unhealthy atmosphere in which probation students and staff sometimes feel unprepared to question the orthodoxy, particularly where race issues are concerned (see Anne Worrall's chapter in this book and Jones, 1993). This is particularly unfortunate in that anti-racist initiatives, in probation as elsewhere, are under constant political attack.

Anti-oppressive practice is included here because it clearly is a value central to contemporary probation practice, enshrined in all the more recent regulations governing professional training although not well defined (e.g. CCETSW, 1991). It might be more accurate to describe it as an emerging value than a fully developed one, and it is impossible to predict the outcome of the debate within probation about its appropriate place, let alone to predict the consequences of the political campaign against anti-oppressive social and probation work.

Despite these reservations, anti-oppressive practice firmly belongs among the core values of probation work. There can be no genuine "respect for persons" without an active commitment to equality of opportunity. Such a commitment in turn entails opposition to what section 95 of the 1991 Criminal Justice Act termed "discrimination on improper grounds". Probation staff are duty bound, by law and professional ethics, to oppose discrimination on the grounds of race, gender, age, disability, educational achievement, literacy or sexual orientation.

It might be argued that probation workers should also oppose discrimination on grounds of class, but this was probably not intended by Parliament. The commitment to oppose oppression does, however, imply that the service must be committed to justice in a more positive sense than merely challenging discrimination. What this might mean in practice is discussed in the rest of this book and in a number of other recent publications (e.g. Dominelli *et al.*, forthcoming; Ward & Lacey, 1994; Sainsbury, 1989). The

13

principle involved can be formulated as follows:

* Probation workers are committed to equality of opportunity, and to justice for all. They oppose oppression and discrimination on the grounds of race, gender, age, disability, educational achievement, literacy or sexual orientation.

* CLIENTS' RIGHT TO CONFIDENTIALITY - AND TO OPENNESS

One of the claims made by professions and occupations aspiring to professional status is that communications between professionals and their clients are covered by an oath of or other commitment to confidentiality. This is both an assertion of the importance of the transactions between the professional and the client, and a claim for professional status (Shardlow, 1991). It usually also arises from the sensitivity of the subjects discussed in the course of consultations with clients, and to that extent it has a purpose and value apart from providing evidence of the worker's status.

Professionals show their respect for clients by protecting confidential information - and they also maintain clients' respect and confidence by doing so. Without trust where confidential information is concerned, there is little hope of a fruitful relationship between any client and professional (see the chapter on throughcare for further discussion of this issue).

Confidentiality figures in any account of social work values (e.g. CCETSW, 1976; Timms, 1989; Jordan, 1993; Butrym, 1976; Biestek, 1961). The discussion of what it means is often very superficial (Shardlow, 1991; Thomas, 1988), as for example in the CCETSW working party document where it occupies a single paragraph. We have already seen that probation officers working with prisoners have developed the concept in a particular way, and this is also discussed further in the chapter on throughcare. Similarly, work with clients diagnosed HIV+ raises particular issues and Una Padel discusses these in her chapter.

It is important that loose thinking about confidentiality is not reflected in workers' dealings with clients, and in this respect the probation service has done something to clarify the practical meaning of the concept. There can be no guarantee that much of the information collected by probation officers in the course of their work will not be transmitted to other parts of officialdom by colleagues, courts and other agencies, particularly in an era where inter-agency partnership has become the norm (see Thomas, 1988). Clients should be warned of this, and by and large they are. There are other constraints, too, in an agency which is part of the criminal justice system. Clients need to be made aware of these; for example, probation officers cannot guarantee to keep information about offences to themselves, or about possible danger to vulnerable people (for example, children).

The other side of confidentiality is the promotion of openness with clients about processes and decisions which affect them. Many professions build up a mystique, and clients find it hard to penetrate. Social work is not immune from this, but probation officers have expanded their understanding of the issue in recent years and have been opening up clients' access to information. There is no need to obfuscate an already obscure process like parole by failing to tell clients what we understand of how decisions are made: it improves professional relationships with clients and shows them respect to share information of this kind (Payne, 1989).

The underlying principle can be stated like this:

* **Probation workers must protect the confidentiality of information about clients, making them aware of the constraints which may make this difficult in practice and giving them a real choice about whether or not to share such information wherever possible. The probation service is also committed to openness with clients about processes and decisions which affect them.**

VALUING CLIENTS AS UNIQUE AND SELF-DETERMINED INDIVIDUALS

Probation officers use social work skills and the humanistic principles which underlie all the caring professions. They show their acceptance of their clients both through the use of learned techniques (such as empathic listening and the conscious display of genuineness, warmth and respect) and through their personal values, which cannot really be learnt, although professional training seeks to clarify them (Williams, 1993).

From the beginnings of social work, respect for individuals has been the cornerstone of its value base. This is not, of course, unique to social work, but it is crucial to its successful practice. As Perlman put it in a discussion of "the diminished man",

". . . if one cannot affirm the worth of the individual man [sic] one cannot affirm the worth of that man multiplied into mankind. . . There is no 'love of mankind' except as fraudulent rhetoric, unless there is compassion for a single human being" (Perlman, 1970, 217).

The Christian origin of the idea shines through her discussion. Her "diminished man" is entitled to respect as a creature of God. An earlier American writer put the idea in a more down to earth way, arguing that the social worker "must consider every individual,

15

however ignorant or dirty or deviant, worthy of respect" (Ferguson, 1963, quoted in Irvine, 1978).

As Eric Sainsbury has pointed out, the police court missionaries worked with people who were rejected by other helping agencies as undeserving. They put the principle of acceptance of clients into practice and set an example (Sainsbury, 1989).

There is a need for an awareness of boundaries where working with offenders is concerned: if one shows acceptance of the client as a human being, how does one also reject aspects of the client's offending behaviour? It is here that the "diminished man" notion is helpful: Perlman's argument is that clients are entitled to self-realisation and self-determination however their disabilities or moral shortcomings may impair their capability. Social workers are there to help them achieve their potential.

We do not need to share the police court missionaries' philosophical framework to see the point of their motto, "love the sinner, hate the sin". One's concern for the client's welfare can be transmitted in the process of dealing with offending. Influencing clients does not impair their capacity for self-determination, but overt control would do so (McDermott, 1975). Parsloe makes the same distinction, with reference to the Government's notion of punishment in the community:

"It is not just a question of semantics, but rather of values to say that social work skills lie in helping people to make informed choices rather than in persuading them." (Parsloe, 1991, 56).

This is absolutely central to the struggle between those who would convert the probation service into a community corrections agency and those who see its social work values as essential to its effectiveness. If probation officers merely exercise control, there is little potential for them to exercise positive influence by helping offenders to make less anti-social decisions.

The underlying principle might be stated as:

* Probation work is based on valuing clients as unique, worthwhile and self-determined individuals. In doing this, social work skills are employed and the principles underlying all the caring professions are involved. In this way, acceptance of clients is communicated. This is kept separate in probation practice from the confronting of offending and offensive behaviour.

VICTIMS AND POTENTIAL VICTIMS OF CRIME ARE PROTECTED

Although, as noted earlier, probation is not the only social work agency which deals with victims of crime, there is a particular dilemma in working with offenders. As social workers who have chosen to specialise in work with an unpopular group, probation officers cannot afford to become too involved in helping the victims of crime. This has been a more noticeable tension since the introduction of Community Service and the involvement of probation staff in the management of victim support schemes. There is scope for conflicts of interest concerning individual cases as well as for disagreements about resourcing.

There is also a dilemma where direct work with offenders is concerned. Offenders and victims of crime are not two discrete groups: in practice, many offenders are themselves crime victims (Peelo *et al.*, 1992). Nevertheless, it has to be made clear to clients that there are certain obligations which override the professional responsibilities to them as offenders. Among these is the legal and ethical requirement to protect the interests of vulnerable people who might become victims.

The probation and social services have a poor record where the victims of "domestic" violence are concerned (Binney *et al.*, 1981; NAPO, 1990; Pahl, 1985; Smith, 1989). In theory, protecting women from such violence should be a higher priority than protecting male clients from prosecution, but there has been a tendency in this country to separate the two issues. In the USA, where this has not been true to the same extent, violent men have been much more likely to be placed in compulsory treatment programmes (Elias, 1993; Stordeur & Stille, 1989). Such schemes are only at an experimental stage in the UK (Swain, 1986; Fagg, 1994).

The balance between clients' interests and those of victims is a difficult one to hold - but it should not be determined by expediency or by collusion with clients. The reasons for probation service involvement with victims of crime may not always be very reputable: although the primary mission of the service is work with offenders and civil work, mandated by the courts, there are strong political reasons for at least a token involvement with victims. As Maguire has pointed out, the decline in belief in the effectiveness of rehabilitation in the 1970s and 1980s led to (or at least coincided with) greater involvement with victims, which "provides an excellent opportunity for demonstrating . . . pursuit of new objectives, such as the promotion of cooperative initiatives in the local community" (Maguire, 1991, 385).

17

Greater awareness of the needs and rights of victims has, however, changed the emphasis of probation work with offenders too. Offence-focused work is likely to be more powerful if it is partly based upon awareness of the impact of offences on their victims, and this awareness makes it harder for criminologists and probation workers to play down the seriousness of crime (Zedner, 1994).

Apart from these general issues, which are very much still subject to debate, the probation service has achieved some consensus about its attitude to victim protection. While the probation officer's main focus is on working with offenders consistently with the other principles we have been discussing, it is agreed that the need to protect victims and potential victims overrides offenders' rights if the risk is serious enough.

Thus, confidentiality may be broken if there is sufficient concern about a child at risk, but probably not where there is anxiety about the danger of a client's partner contracting AIDS (see the discussion in Una Padel's chapter of the latter issue). Practice in such matters cannot be guided by abstract rules, and complex issues have to be balanced when making decisions of this kind. What is important is that victim awareness is on the agenda during supervision of clients and more generally, without necessarily altering fundamentally the mission of the probation service. In North America, the political pressure on behalf of (or rather, in the name of) victims has upset this balance without making matters any better for the victims: they have been used as a political football (Elias, 1993).

The general principle for probation workers might be formulated thus:

*The need to protect victims and potential victims of crime must be balanced against the rights and needs of offenders under supervision. In certain circumstances, where the risk to victims is serious enough, victim protection overrides offenders' rights.

PURPOSEFUL PROFESSIONAL RELATIONSHIPS CAN FACILITATE CHANGE IN CLIENTS

Again, the Christian origins of social work have been influential on modern professional values. The idea of saving souls, helping individuals earn their place in heaven, has been modified over the decades of social work practice. Police court missionaries argued with the Church as to whether some modest improvement in clients' behaviour was a step in the right direction, or whether total abstinence and law-abiding behaviour should always be advocated. The softer, "meliorist" line prevailed (McWilliams 1983). This meant that probation officers could accept the notion of a "relapse cycle" (see Andrew Shephard's chapter) rather than preaching the need for total abstinence where alcohol was concerned, and this distinction can be transferred to other areas of probation work. The robber who takes up shoplifting has made progress, and in a sentencing framework supposedly based upon the seriousness of the offence currently before the court, this should be seen as a mitigating factor.

Despite all the agonising about whether rehabilitation was effective during the 1980s and early 1990s, modern probation work is based upon the beliefs that clients' behaviour can change for the better and that probation officers can influence this. Recent research has given grounds for some optimism about the effectiveness of probation work, broadly defined, if it is systematic and selective, in influencing the levels of clients' offending (Raynor *et al.*, 1994).

There is always a danger that such a definition of effectiveness is seen as manipulative and patronising. Indeed, many of the principles outlined above are open to such an interpretation. The concern to avoid manipulation of clients can be met to some extent by openness between probation workers and their clients about the aims of intervention, but this too can be manipulated if operated in a cynical or bureaucratic way. Only if the social work methods mentioned earlier - warmth, empathy, real listening - are used and taken to heart, and combined with a concern for justice, will it be possible to influence clients positively. One of the major points of the research on what works is that there is no rehabilitative technology which can be removed from its context in a personal relationship bounded by humanistic values.

Probation workers have to believe that clients can change, and that some of them want to do so, at least part of the time. This is not only because such a belief sustains morale (the work would be pointless without it), but because we know, and clients know, that the consequences of repeated offending are progressively destructive responses from the criminal justice system. One way of avoiding paternalistic practice is to ensure that the probation service responds to client needs - and this is also an identified feature of effective work (McIvor, 1990). The clear failure of custodial institutions to rehabilitate offenders points to one client need which has already been discussed at some length: the need for credible community-based disposals which have constructive outcomes.

As with the example, given above, of meliorist practice and later awareness of the concept of a relapse cycle, effective probation practice is well informed. For too long, probation officers have been suspicious of criminological research findings (perhaps partly because of the misunderstandings which led to a widespread belief that the research said that "nothing works" (Raynor, 1985), when what it actually said was much more subtle and complex). Clients have a right to expect that probation workers will be well informed as to what is likely to work. In the end, though, successful probation practitioners seem likely to be the ones who are interested in the outcomes of their interventions (Raynor *et al.*, 1994).

It seems clear that some types of offender are more receptive to probation intervention than others, and that some patterns of offending behaviour are very much more difficult to change than others: repeated sexual offending against children is harder to challenge effectively than repeated indecent exposure, for example. This is partly a matter of client motivation: if an offender sees nothing wrong with his behaviour, his motivation to change is likely to be focused mainly upon the unpleasant consequences of detection. This means not that the belief in clients' capacity to change is no longer relevant, but that it has to be tempered with realism and tested out with individual offenders. To fail to accept that some recidivists want to change would be a counsel of despair. I have argued elsewhere (Williams, 1991, 1992) that the crucial issue is the kind of relationships that are formed between clients and workers, and there is no need to repeat those arguments here. They are implicit in much of the remainder of this book.

To summarise, the final practice principle put forward here is:

* Probation workers base their work on the assumption that offenders can change, that recidivism is not inevitable, and that the nature of professional relationships with clients is influential.

In the chapters that follow, the authors examine these principles in a variety of ways in relation to specific areas of practice and particular client groups.

In Chapter Two, Anne Worrall examines the rhetoric of equal opportunities in the probation service and some of the reasons for failures in implementation. She looks at the uncritical and depoliticised ways in which inequality and discrimination have traditionally been discussed, and argues against the "received wisdom" which has inhibited honest debate.

Bill Beaumont, in Chapter Three, analyses the development of managerialism in the probation service and notes the lack of "fit" between the underlying values of the management theories espoused by much of the probation service and the social work values they attempted to displace. The effects upon the workforce are tellingly examined, from the perspective of a former general secretary of NAPO.

The next chapter, by Bill Jordan and Jon Arnold, considers the relationship between probation values, the training of probation officers and wider issues of social justice. The historical and philosophical origins of present-day probation values are used to focus on the current conflicts between probation training and the dominant ideology.

The book then moves from general issues to consider specialised areas of practice, beginning with the most common. In Chapter Five, Anne Celnick and Bill McWilliams use examples of court reports to illustrate some of the conflicts between justice and values in practice. Using national standards as a case study, they show that PSRs may represent an advance on SERs in terms of the service provided both to defendants and to courts, but that important ethical issues have first to be clarified.

In Chapter Six, I outline the relevance of probation values to probation work with prisoners, giving some examples of the conflicts which arise between a relatively optimistic, mainly community-based probation service and the largely closed world of the prisons, which have little time for rehabilitative optimism.

Andrew Shephard discusses some of the professional controversies relating to alcohol and drug misuse in Chapter Seven. A hypothetical probation team is taken through the attractions and difficulties of a number of possible approaches to working with clients who are substance misusers, and the possibilities arising from current Government policy on partnerships are considered in relation to this area of work.

Chapter Eight, by Una Padel, looks at the issues arising from HIV and AIDS. She briefly reviews policy responses to the epidemic, and then moves on to consider practice issues, including some of those discussed from other perspectives in earlier chapters. HIV illustrates very effectively the challenges to professional values, and the chapter poses many dilemmas, offering practical solutions to most of them.

Finally, Bryan Gocke looks at the difficulties of respecting clients' rights and needs in an area of work where victims' rights and needs may need to be paramount: work with sexual offenders.

He notes the dynamic relationship between research on such offenders and practitioners' values, which have changed to reflect the realities of this area of work. Some of the tensions and contradictions between agencies' stated principles and values, those of the wider criminal justice system on the one hand and those of the individual practitioner on the other, are examined from a researcher and practitioner perspective. In my view, he succeeds in showing that the value base outlined earlier in the book is useful even in areas of work which call it into question constantly. He treats sex offenders as a group which challenges received opinions about the underlying values of probation work, and identifies work which needs to be done - starting now, to develop appropriate values for this group.

[1] The head of the probation inspectorate was presumably well aware of the implications when, in his annual report for 1992-3, he used the phrase "community corrections" (HMIP, 1993: 9). This may prove to have been politically astute, but at the time it appeared simply to be pandering to "just deserts" extremists in the Conservative Party.

[2] The 1994 reworking of this document formed part of the basis of a revised paper 30 (setting out the competences for social work qualifying training). It is a sign of the times that it was prepared not by a working party of CCETSW, but by a firm of consultants. They met once with probation interests during the "values" exercise, and had clearly not come across the earlier CCETSW paper.

[3] During the summer of 1993, there was a concerted media campaign against the "political correctness" of the social work profession, which focused on the "notorious Paper 30, a dry list of competences which none of the journalists appeared to have read. This was largely directed against the "loony" observation that Britain is characterised by structural inequalities and in particular institutionalised racism. By the autumn of that year, CCETSW had returned to the rhetoric of "equal opportunities" and "anti-discriminatory practice", which must have seemed safer in the face of a hostile Home Office and Department of Health (see Jones, 1993; Pinker, 1993).

References

Ahmed, S. "Developing anti-racist social work education practice" in (ed.) Curriculum Development Project Steering Group, *Setting the context for change*, CCETSW, 1991

Bentham, J. *An introduction to the principles of morals and legislation*, Athlone Press, 1970 (eds. J. H. Burns & H. L. A. Hart)

Biestek, F. *The casework relationship*, Allen & Unwin, 1961

Biggs, S. "Case management and inspection", *Critical Social Policy* 30 1990

Binney, V. Harkell, G & Nixon, N. *Leaving violent men*, Women's Aid Federation England, 1981

Bochel, D. *Probation and after-care: its development in England and Wales*, Edinburgh: Scottish Academic Press, 1976

British Association of Social Workers, *A code of ethics for social workers*, Birmingham: BASW Publications, 1975, revised 1986

Butrym, Z. *The nature of social work*, Macmillan, 1976

Campaign Against Double Punishment, *No immigration laws, no double punishment*, Manchester: CADP, 1992

Central Council for the Education and Training of Social Workers, *Values in social work*, CCETSW Paper 13, CCETSW, 1976

CCETSW, *Rules and requirements for the Diploma in Social Work*, CCETSW Paper 30, CCETSW, 1991

The Children's Society, *The case against locking up more children*, Children's Society, 1993

Christie, N. *Crime control as industry*, Routledge, 1993

Divine, D. "The value of anti-racism in social work education and training", in (ed.) Curriculum Development Project Steering Group, *Setting the context for change*, CCETSW, 1991

Dominelli, D. Jeffers, L. Jones, G. Sibanda, S & Williams, B. *Anti-racist probation practice*, Aldershot: Arena, forthcoming 1995

Drakeford, M. "But who will do the work?", *Critical Social Policy* 38 1993 64-76 (1993a)

Drakeford, M. "The probation service, breach and the Criminal Justice Act 1991", *Howard Journal* 32 (4) 1993 291-303

Elias, R. *Victims still: the political manipulation of crime victims*, Sage, 1993

Fagg, C. "To what extent does the male socialisation process provide an explanation for violence within intimate relationships? Does society (specifically the probation service) have a responsibility to confront this issue?", unpublished MA thesis, Department of Sociological Studies, University of Sheffield, Sheffield, 1994

Goldson, B. "The changing face of youth justice", *Childright* 105 1994 5-6

Hale, J. "Feminism in social work practice", in (eds.) Jordan, B & Parton, N. *The political dimensions of social work*, Oxford: Basil Blackwell, 1983

Hardy, J. *Values in social policy: nine contradictions,* Routledge Kegan Paul, 1981

HM Inspectorate of Probation, *Annual Report 1992-93*, HMSO, 1993

Home Office, *Crime, justice and protecting the public*, HMSO, Cm. 965

Irvine, E, E. "Professional claims and the professional task" in Social Sciences: a second level course, *Professional and non-professional roles 1,* Milton Keynes: Open University Press, 1978

Jones, C. "Distortion and demonisation: the right and anti-racist social work education", *Social Work Education 12* (3) 1993 9-16

Jordan, B., Karban, K., Kazi, M., Masson, H. & O'Byrne, P. "Teaching values: an experience of the Diploma in Social Work", *Social Work Education 12* (1) 1993 7-18

Kett, J. *et al.*, *Managing and developing anti-racist practice within probation, a resource pack for action*, St Helens: Merseyside Probation Service, 1992

Lipsky, M. "The assault on human services: street-level bureaucrats, accountability and the fiscal crisis", in (eds.) Scott Greer, Ronald Hedlund & James L Gibson, *Accountability in urban societies: public agencies under fire*, Sage 1978

Maguire, M. "The needs and rights of victims of crime", *Crime and Justice, a Review of Research*, 14, 1991, 363-433

McDermott, F. E. *Self-determination in social work*, RKP, 1975

McIvor, G. *Sanctions for serious or persistent offenders: a review of the literature*, Stirling: Social Work Research Centre, University of Stirling

McWilliams, B. "The mission to the English police courts 1876-1936", *Howard Journal* 22 (3) 1983 129-47

McWilliams, B. "The rise and development of management thought in the English probation service", in (eds.) Statham, R & Whitehead, P. *Managing the probation service*, Harlow: Longman, 1992

Monger, M. *Casework in probation*, Butterworths, 1972

Morris, P. & Beverly, F. *On licence: a study of parole*, Wiley, 1975

National Association for the Care and Resettlement of Offenders, *Race policies into action, the implementation of equal opportunities policies in criminal justice agencies*, Report of the NACRO Race Issues Advisory Committee, NACRO, 1992

National Association of Probation Officers, "Advice/information for women about to start prison secondments - some strategies for survival", Trade Union Organisation Committee paper TUO41/91, mimeo, NAPO, 1991

National Association of Probation Officers, "Work with men who abuse women and/or children - guidelines for branch negotiation", Probation Practice Committee paper pp22/90, mimeo, NAPO, 1990

Nellis, M. "Criminology, crime prevention and the future of probation training", in (eds.) Keith Bottomley, Tony Fowles & Robert Reiner, *Criminal justice: theory and practice*, British Criminology Conference 1991 Selected Papers volume 2, BSC/ISTD, 1993

Nellis, M. "The last days of 'juvenile' justice?", in (eds.) Pam Carter *et al.*, *Social Work and Social Welfare* 3, Milton Keynes: Open University Press, 1991

Nellis, M. "Towards a new view of probation values", in (eds.) Richard Hugman & David Smith, *Ethics and social work*, Routledge, forthcoming, 1995

Nellis, M. "What is to be done about probation training?", in (eds.) Tim May & Tony Vass, *Working with offenders* (provisional title), forthcoming, 1995a

New Approaches to Juvenile Crime, *Creating more criminals: the case against a new 'secure training order' for juvenile offenders*, NAJC, 1994

Pahl, J. (ed.), *Private violence and public policy: the needs of battered women and the response of the public services*, Routledge & Kegan Paul, 1985

Parsloe, P. "What is probation?", *Social Work Education* 10 (2) 1991 50-59

Payne, M. "Open records and shared decisions with clients", in (ed.) Shardlow, S. *The values of change in social work*, Tavistock/Routledge, 1989

Peelo, M., Stewart, J., Stewart, G .& Prior, A. *A sense of justice: offenders as victims of crime*, Wakefield: ACOP, 1992

Perlman, H. "Casework and 'the diminished man'", *Social Casework 51* (4) 1970 216-24

Pinker, R. "A lethal dose of looniness", *Times Higher Education Supplement*, 10 September 1993

Pitts, J. *The politics of juvenile crime*, Sage, 1988

Raynor, P. *Social work, justice and control,* Oxford: Blackwell, 1985

Raynor, P., Smith, D. & Vanstone, M. *Effective probation practice, Macmillan*, 1994

Rojek, C., Peacock, G. & Collins,S. *Social work and received ideas*, Routledge, 1988

Rutherford, A. *Growing out of crime: the new era*, 2nd ed., Winchester: Waterside, 1992

Sainsbury, E. "Participation and paternalism" in (ed.) Shardlow, S. *The values of change in social work*, Tavistock/Routledge, 1989

Shardlow, S. "Inspecting social work values", *Practice 5* (1) 1991 76-85

Simon, J. *Poor discipline: parole and the social control of the underclass, 1890-1990*, University of Chicago Press, 1993

Smith, L. J. *Domestic violence: an overview of the literature*, Home Office Research Study 107, Home Office, 1989

Stordeur, R. A & Stille, R. *Ending men's violence against their partners*, Sage, 1989

Swain, K. "Probation attitudes to battered women: apathy, error and avoidance", *Probation Journal*, 33 (4) 132-4

Thomas, R. & Vanstone, M. "Leadership in the middle", *Probation Journal* 39 (1) 1992 19-23

Thomas, T. "Confidentiality: the loss of a concept?", *Practice 2* (4) 1988 358-72

Timms, N. *Social work values: an enquiry*, Routledge Kegan Paul, 1983

Timms, N. "Social work values: context and contribution", in (ed.) Shardlow, S. *The values of change in social work*, Tavistock/Routledge, 1989

Travis, A. "Ex-soldiers sought to beef up probation", *The Guardian*, 27 June 1994

Varah, M. "Probation and community service", in (ed.)Harding, J. *Probation and the community*, Tavistock, 1987

Walker, H. & Beaumont, B. *Probation work: critical theory and socialist practice*, Oxford: Basil Blackwell, 1981

Ward, D. & Spencer, J. 'The future of probation qualifying training", *Probation Journal* 41 (2) 1994 95-8

Ward, D. & Lacey, M. (eds) *Towards greater justice*, Whiting & Birch, 1995

Williams, B. "Caring professionals or street-level bureaucrats? The case of probation officers' work with prisoners", *Howard Journal* 31 (4) 1992 263-75

Williams, B. "The transition from prison to community", in (eds.) May, T. & Vass, T. *Working with offenders* (provisional title), Sage, forthcoming 1995

Williams, B. "What is happening to prison education?", *Prison Writing 1* (2) 1993 40-56

Williams, B. "Towards justice in probation work with prisoners", in (eds.) Ward, D. & Lacey, M. *Towards greater justice*, Whiting & Birch, 1995

Williams, B. *Work with prisoners*, Birmingham: Venture, 1991

Williams, B. "Social work values in the criminal justice system", paper delivered at the BASW conference on Social work values within a correctional system, Stirling, 1993

Zedner, L. "Victims", in (eds) Maguire, M. Morgan, R. & Reiner, R. *The Oxford handbook of criminology*, Clarendon, Oxford, 1994

TWO:
EQUAL OPPORTUNITY OR EQUAL DISILLUSION? THE PROBATION SERVICE AND ANTI-DISCRIMINATOR PRACTICE

Anne Worrall

"Our lives are suspended between the recognition of personal difference and the yearning to be close to everyone else."

(Rojek, Peacock and Collins, 1988:116)

The discourse of anti-discriminatory practice[1] is relatively new to social work, having emerged over the last ten years and having now become the corner-stone of social work and probation training. The construction of such ideas as marking a radical departure from previous ideological underpinnings has shaken social work out of its apolitical complacency. But there is a danger that, by emphasising the newness of ideas, they become detached from their historical roots and are reified as unquestionable creeds or, worse, flavours of the month that fade as quickly as they arrived. Thus intellectually 'gutted', they are exposed to the kind of right-wing media 'distortion and demonisation' which social work experienced in the summer of 1993 (Jones, 1993).

The aim of this chapter is to explore the relationship between the rhetoric and reality of anti-discriminatory practice and equal opportunities policies in the Probation Service. It will set such a discussion in the context of the development of values discourse in social work and will seek to put forward the following arguments:

1. Anti-discriminatory practice is the most recent manifestation of social work's deep-seated concern for people who are placed at a disadvantage by virtue of structural inequalities in society. As such, it needs to be informed more by open-minded historical and sociological analyses than by restrictive dogma.

2. Despite a greatly increased awareness of the discrimination experienced by black[2] offenders, service delivery has failed to reduce their disproportionate numbers in prison because of a shared lack of confidence amongst probation officers and black offenders that the Probation Service has anything to offer.

3. Despite a greatly increased awareness of the (different) discrimination experienced by white female offenders, service delivery has failed to prevent their inappropriate imprisonment because of a partially successful policy of minimal intervention which has nevertheless left certain women 'at risk' of custody but abandoned by the Service.

4. Equal opportunities employment policies which emphasise the achievement of formal justice through procedural clarity and explicit objective-setting may thereby sacrifice substantive justice, which can only be achieved through a recognition of complexity, uncertainty and incompleteness.

SOCIAL WORK AND DIFFERENCE

It is important to understand how and why discrimination became such an issue in social work and that requires, as a pre-condition, the exploration of the ways in which social work has interpreted and handled the concept of difference. The ideology of social work has always been concerned with social difference and with helping disadvantaged individuals to function better within society. In the past, however, it has tended to avoid critical examination of why individuals are disadvantaged and what is meant by "function better in society". In short, it has avoided critical discussion of power, structural inequality and discrimination within society.

Nevertheless, there are several concepts which have been categorised as 'traditional social work values' which are relevant to the discussion of difference. Respect for persons (Biestek, 1961) implies that every individual is of worth, regardless of their race, gender, class, age or status and that every individual has a right to an equal professional social work service. Linked with this are notions of acceptance and non-judgemental attitudes (Biestek, 1961). However different a person's biography or behaviour, the job of the social worker and probation officer is to understand and accept as valid that person's life situation, without judgement or condemnation.

If respect for persons is one of the key values of social work, then the means of demonstrating this value is through the exercise of empathy. Empathy is the most ubiquitous cliché in social work jargon. Rarely defined, it commands the same uncritical acclaim within the profession as appeals to common sense do amongst magistrates and politicians. The appeal of empathy lies in the reassurance it affords social workers that there is common ground between them and the people they are authorised to care for or control. But the question that is invariably begged when we claim to be "entering the world" of another person is whether we succeed in empathising with them by relying on what we appear to have in common with them or by recognising the differences between us.

TRADITIONAL SOCIAL WORK AND INDIVIDUALISATION

The history of social work has been a history of the conflict between these two interpretations of the nature of the social work relationship. Within the language and vocabulary of traditional professional social work, empathy derives its meaning within the context of an emphasis on individualisation and the uniqueness of every person's experience. Any claim to common characteristics or common experience between worker and service user is dismissed as being both illusory and dangerous. It is illusory because we can never understand exactly what an experience means to another person even if we seem to have been through the same experience objectively, or to have the same objective characteristic (such as age, gender or race). It is dangerous because, if we base our understanding of others on what we seem to have in common with them, then we are likely to be limited in our vision of their needs and blocked in our ability to help them. It may be attractive and tempting to say to a service user "I know what you mean because I've been through it too" and it may give the user a welcome sense of normality and shared humanity at a superficial level but the logical conclusion of those sentiments is that the worker's solution ought also to be the user's solution.

So traditional social work has emphasised the need for professional detachment and the avoidance of spurious "common sense" solutions. It has set great store by the acquisition of knowledge and the learning of value-neutral techniques of helping. These are communicated to the client through a carefully cultivated professional relationship which transcends personal and social difference. It doesn't matter, for example, that you as a user are a woman and I as a worker am a man because the professional relationship is gender-neutral and, even if I were a woman, that wouldn't mean that I understood any better what being a woman means to you. I understand your problems precisely because they are different from mine. I use my informed imagination to understand what it feels like for you.

In fact, any similar experience I may think I have may in fact inhibit rather than assist that process of understanding. The Probation Service has always had mixed feelings about identifying itself with traditional social work, arguing that the controlling aspects of its work and the legal framework within which it operates set it apart. Haxby (1978), however, who is often credited with being the pioneer of "community corrections" thinking in the Probation Service, demonstrated that the differences between probation officers and, for example, social workers in child care, were far less marked than probation officers claimed. Furthermore, he argued strongly for probation officers to retain a professional identity as social workers in order to resist pressure to undertake inappropriate tasks:

"If social work within the criminal justice system is not to be distorted by legislators and administrators to serve punitive or regulatory purposes, there must be clear identification by probation officers with a professional group which will express its concern, from outside the agency, if the tasks they are asked to undertake violate approved principles or values of social work practice."

(Haxby, 1978: 121)

RADICAL SOCIAL WORK AND CONSCIOUSNESS

But the word "empathy" disappeared from social work vocabulary in the hey-day of Marxist social work. It was rejected as being a euphemism for the regulation of the service user. Emphasis on individualisation and the uniqueness of individual experience was seen as one of the ways in which the state, through its ideological apparatuses, maintained existing social structures to the benefit of capitalism (Rojek, Peacock and Collins, 1988). The result was the alienation of a whole underclass in society, euphemistically referred to as "clients".

The pessimistic view of social work was that it was an indispensable part of the capitalist state machine. It functioned to produce, maintain and reproduce working-class subordination. Social workers were the soft cops of the capitalist state. The more optimistic view was that social work could bring about social change and the understanding of difference but only by abandoning its pseudo-scientific vocabulary and its focus on individual pathology. (Bailey and Brake, 1975; Corrigan and Leonard, 1978)

So the key to understanding difference in the context of radical socialist social work was not empathy but consciousness. Consciousness was based on the assumption that certain experiences, particularly those of class, are shared objectively and should be shared subjectively. It is only through this sharing that people can start to help each other in relationships of equality and reciprocity. Help is more likely to be effective if it comes from someone in a similar position to you - hence the development of self-help groups.

This left the social worker with two options: first, to acknowledge the power differential and use it to facilitate and advocate for self-help groups - to be the servant rather than the doctor; and/or, second, to identify with clients as fellow workers and employees of the state and form alliances through the trades union movement to effect wider social change.

Within the Probation Service, radical social work was most apparent in the development of the National Association of Probation Officers as a trade union in the 1970s. Politically increasingly left wing, it campaigned on ideological grounds to withdraw from prisons, to refuse to write social inquiry reports in "not guilty" pleas and for the right to demonstrate in solidarity with workers not directly concerned with criminal justice (participation in the Grunwick dispute leading to the suspension from NAPO of its London branch). Bitter wranglings over the issue of *ultra vires* led to new objectives to extend the legitimate interests of NAPO to concern about social as well as criminal justice.

By the early 1980s (arguably when the political tide had already turned against it) the Probation Service had its own book on radical social work in the form of Walker and Beaumont's influential Probation Work: Critical Theory and Socialist Practice (1981). Less overtly subversive but perhaps even more influential in practice was the article by Bottoms and McWilliams, "A non-treatment paradigm for probation practice" (1979) which sought to balance the care and control elements of the job whilst discarding the pseudo-medical vocabulary of rehabilitation.

FEMINIST SOCIAL WORK: THE PERSONAL IS POLITICAL

Many criticisms have been levelled at Marxist social work but for the purposes of this exploration, attention can be focused on

a) its neglect of the immediate personal needs of users in favour of promoting consciousness or some form of collective action;

b) its neglect of emotional problems in favour of concentration on material and social issues;

c) its neglect of power differentials in personal relationships in favour of concentration on class power and

d) its neglect of women.

Radical social work was the "angry young man's terrain" (Rojek, Peacock & Collins, 1988: 84). It had a "macho", revolutionary image which seemed to ignore the fact that most social workers and service users are women.

By contrast, feminist social work challenged received wisdom about women's needs (Hudson, 1985). It redefined women's problems in terms of their common oppression rather than their individual inadequacy or emotional instability. It highlighted the need for special resources for women, initially in relation to their needs as victims of male violence but then in relation to mental health, criminal justice and local authority care. It challenged the myth of gender-neutral provision - the assumption that men and women have equal access to and take equal advantage of provision. It exposed the dangers of the family. Traditional and radical social work both constructed the family as a potential haven from the conflicts of the outside world. Feminism demonstrated that the family is not a safe place for many women and children. Finally, it suggested (controversially) that women could only be helped by other women. It challenged the traditional notion of empathy as an expression of acknowledged difference and suggested that it had to have its roots in a shared experience of gender oppression.

The impact of criminology on the Probation Service has perhaps been at its greatest in relation to women offenders. Academics who have never worked in the Service, such as Carol Smart (1976), Pat Carlen (1983,1985,1988,1990), Frances Heidensohn (1985) and Mary Eaton (1986,1993) have been read and quoted by a generation of probation officers to an extent unmatched, I would suggest, by any other academic writer in the criminal justice field. The contribution of such work to the Service's understanding of women offenders and its work with them has been highly significant (Worrall, 1993; 1995). Of particular relevance to this discussion has been the breaking down of traditional barriers and the realisation of partnership between women workers in the criminal justice system, women criminologists and women offenders to raise awareness, campaign and provide imaginative resources for women offenders.

Despite this, it has become apparent that, although gender-consciousness has been very successful in diverting (predominantly white) women who have committed minor offences away from the criminal justice system (numbers of women placed on probation have fallen dramatically over the past decade - see Worrall, 1993, 1995), it has failed to make any impact at the other end of what used to be termed the "tariff". Failure to keep more women out of prison may be due, at least in part, to a misrecognition of when women offenders are "at risk" of custody.

We know that women tend go to prison earlier in their criminal

34

careers and for less serious offences than men. Yet strict adherence to an "anti-discriminatory" policy of minimal intervention may lead probation officers to refuse to refer certain (often black?) women to Probation Centres or for Community Service, with the result that they end up in prison by default.

Although feminist social work has been predominantly concerned with women, its influence has been broader. By placing gender on the social work agenda it has slowly encouraged men to look at their own sexuality and the social construction of masculinity (Hudson, 1988; Cordery & Whitehead, 1992; McCaughey, 1992). It has opened up the debate about how to work with violent and sexual offenders. It has championed the cause of equal opportunities and has thereby legitimated the voices of other oppressed groups. It has forged a link between the individualism of traditional social work and the politics of radical social work by arguing that what happens in people's personal lives and how they struggle individually are making a political statement.

ANTI-RACIST SOCIAL WORK: HIERARCHIES OF DISCRIMINATION?

It is against this backdrop of debate about the nature of social work and the beginning of post-modernist attempts at deconstruction (Rojek, Peacock and Collins, 1988) that the emergence of anti-racist social work in the late 1980s has to be viewed. In an attempt to move beyond the multi-culturalism which had placed intolerable burdens on token black professionals whilst leaving the attitudes, behaviour and policies of liberal white professionals unchallenged, CCETSW insisted that all aspiring DipSW programmes should demonstrate their commitment to anti-racist social work practice. It was a bold and necessary move but many interpreted it as establishing a hierarchy of discrimination which could only be disputed at one's peril (approval was withheld from some programmes that argued against the separation of anti-racism from other forms of discrimination). A new "totalising schema" appeared (Pitts, 1993).

One particular discourse of resistance became privileged and institutionalised, the paradoxical consequences of which have reverberated throughout the profession. The liberation afforded by a post-modernist interrogation which insists that nothing is certain or coherent and that everything can and should be questioned appeared to be denied when it came to racism. Whilst much was achieved by confronting the profession with its own complacency, the worst excesses of the "anti-racism industry" (Pitts, 1993) within social work did precisely what Gilroy (1987) had warned against. It had the effect ".... of appearing to reduce the complexity of black life to an effect of racism. This is a real danger when racism is presented sweeping all before it and the power relations involved are caricatured as an eternal tussle between victims and perpetrators". (Gilroy, 1987:150)

Thus the spectre of received wisdom returned with almost unbearable irony, for it played into the hands of those who were only too happy to foreclose on any debate and go "back to basics" - the "basics" being the creation of a "bureaucratically compliant workforce", de-intellectualised and deprofessionalised (Jones, 1993).

The impact of racism in the criminal justice system had already become blatantly obvious. Research study after research study demonstrated that young black men were more likely to be stopped and searched, less likely to be cautioned, more likely to be referred for reports but less likely to receive non-custodial recommendations and sentences than their white counterparts. Discrimination was seen to be cumulative rather than specific at any one stage of the process but probation officers were undoubtedly making a significant contribution. Unlike studies on women offenders, however, there seemed to be little attempt to draw on mainstream criminology or criminologists to explore what was happening. The level of analysis was simplistic - either black people were actually committing more crime than white people, as a result of their experiences of racism, or racism was responsible for constructing black people as being more criminal than white people. Either way, the focus was on social reaction rather than an exploration of aetiology. Two notable exceptions have been the work of John Pitts (1986,1993) who has consistently rooted discussion of racism in broader understandings about youth justice and social inequality, and David Denney (1992) who has utilised discourse analysis to deconstruct professional assessments of black offenders and to provide insight into the difficulties which (white) probation officers have in transforming black offenders into "the 'good subject' who can be conceptualised as having the 'potential' to become structured into and identify with probation discourses". (Denney, 1992:128)

Anti-discriminatory social work is rooted in, and has evolved from, traditional social work values. It is also connected with postmodern concerns with the significance of difference and uncertainty. Unless it retains its openness to the nourishment provided by these discourses, it will either wither and die under the weight of political and media distortion or find itself (mis)appropriated into the rhetoric of formalised equal opportunity policies, by organisations which are (self-) satisfied merely to increase access to its always-already-known modernist ideology of certainty and homo-geneity. As Pitts argues: "When confronted with problems which, in an earlier era, had been attributed to 'social injustice', welfare and justice agencies, in managerialist mode, simply developed equal opportunities policies and talked about 'targeting'. Thus structural inequalities were transformed into administrative anomalies for which bureaucratic solutions could be devised." (Pitts, 1993: 103)

EQUAL OPPORTUNITIES POLICIES AND ORGANISATIONAL CULTURE: WHITE WOMEN WORKING IN THE PROBATION SERVICE

It is perhaps no accident that a recent book on the management of the Probation Service in the 1990s (Statham and Whitehead, 1992) contains no more than a few passing references to equal opportunities and one short section concerned exclusively with the rights of offenders "to citizenship and access to political, social and economic opportunities like the rest of us" (1992:184, emphasis added). The debate about management in the service, unlike that in relation to many other organisations, including social services, is conducted in almost entirely gender-neutral terms. There is no Probation Service equivalent of the Department of Health Social Services Inspectorate Report Women in the Social Services: a Neglected Resource (1991), which acknowledges the growing body of evidence that women workers are alienated by and from a manage-ment culture which they experience as devaluing and undermining the qualities and attributes which they bring to the organisation.

Consistent themes emerge from studies of women working in organisations (Wells, 1983; Walby, 1987; Coleman, 1991; Merchant, 1993). The first of these is the awareness of difference, of being out of sympathy with the prevailing "style" and value system of the organisation. Women tend to judge themselves by their own internal and often exacting standards, rather than by the overt standards of the organisation. Secondly, they withdraw from or avoid tasks or situations where they anticipate conflict as a consequence of being female. The cumulative effect of this is a self-imposed restriction on personal development and on opportunities to meet new people and undertake new tasks. A third theme is the impact of having children and the extent to which child care over-whelmingly remains a female responsibility. Two final themes concern styles of working and communication. Women workers are typically portrayed as preferring to focus on relationships and processes, whilst male colleagues are seen to be more task- and outcome-oriented, the latter reflecting more accurately the overall ethos of the organisation and the approbated qualities of its employees. Finally, women find themselves alienated from the dominant communication system in the organisation. Men, it is argued, place more value on articulacy and "objective" knowledge, rejecting the communication of the intuitive and the experiential, which frequently appears less certain or complete. To use Ardener's inspirational concept, women are "muted":

> *"The theory of mutedness . . . does not require that the muted be actually silent. They may speak a great deal. The important issue is whether they are able to say all they would wish to say, where and when they wish to say it. Must they, for instance, re-encode their thoughts to make them understood in the public domain? Are they able to think in ways which they would have thought had they been responsible for generating the linguistic tools with which to shape their thoughts? If they devise their own code will they be understood?"*
>
> (Ardener, 1978:21)

None of this is intended to support the positivistic argument that women are essentially more communal and less "agentic" than men (Hayles, 1989). It is simplistic to say that women's "overriding objective is wholeness, a rounded life-style" whereas men "pursue single-mindedly one particular goal such as career success" (Hayles, 1989;14). It is the burdening of men and women with such myths and stereotypes that compounds the polarisation of the genders and allows male managers to project (and dismiss) certain aspects of themselves and their organisation on to their female colleagues. The analysis with which we have to engage is that of the organisation itself and, in particular, the relationship between the formal and the informal (Cooper and Burrell, 1988). The "formal" character of an organisation is its rational authority, its official discourse, the ways in which it defines and publicly presents its role and the roles of its employees. The "informal" character (which is inescapably connected to the "formal") is everything which threatens to transgress the "formal", everything which blurs boundaries and confuses roles, everything which is familiar and intimate. For example, the following quotation from Promoting Women (Allan, Bhavnani & French, 1992) illustrates the extent to which equal opportunities interviewing can act as a barrier to promotion:

> *"Interviews were described by women in several (Social Services) authorities as being rigid and formal. They felt intimidated by the process characterised by a lack of expression by interviewers, and that flat faces giving no feedback*

did not encourage further discussion. Single questions were asked with no follow up around that area of inquiry. Women experienced the rigid formality of the resulting process as one which reduced their ability to demonstrate their knowledge and skills. "

(Allan, Bhavnani & French, 1992:14)

It is only when we begin to explore this relationship between the formal and the informal that we will uncover the mechanisms whereby organisations (and the Probation Service in particular) interpret and handle difference, whether that be gender, race, age or any other manifestation of difference.

BLACK MEN AND WOMEN WORKING IN THE PROBATION SERVICE

It would be an error to suggest that black people experience the same obstacles as white women working in organisations. There is evidence that black people are highly committed to the promotion of formal equal opportunities policies and that black women sometimes feel that such policies are more significant for them from a race than a gender perspective (Allan, Bhavnani & French, 1992). Whilst critical of their implementation, black people see the way forward as lying in greater explicitness and procedural clarity (NACRO, 1992).

Recruitment and retention of white women as main-grade probation officers are not a problem for the organisation, since 50 per cent of that workforce is now female (Merchant, 1993). With less than 3 per cent of main-grade officers identifying themselves as black (Home Office, 1992) the emphasis on recruitment and retention practices is far more crucial. NACRO (1992) identifies four obstacles which need to be overcome if black people are to be proportionately represented as employees in the Service. First, there is a need to overcome the perception that the service is part of a system which oppresses black people, as evidenced by their dispro-portionate numbers in prison. For this reason, equal opportunities recruitment policies cannot be separated from broader issues of anti-racist service delivery. Second, there is a need to find ways of redressing cumulative educational disadvantage which tends to render disproportionate numbers of black people ineligible for qualifying training. Without compromising standards, less conven-tional routes to meeting entry criteria need to be explored. Third, recruitment procedures and selection criteria which are fair and relevant - at every stage - to the position being applied for need to be in use and seen to be in use. But, fourth, none of these provisions (which are essentially provisions to improve communication with black people) will be sufficient to retain black staff unless they feel that a) the job is worth doing and b) the working environment is supportive and free from discrimination.

ORGANISING DIFFERENCE

The very term "organisation" implies a disciplinary enterprise, a desire to reduce difference to sameness, to minimise the risk of discrepancy, inconsistency and incongruity. The function of the organisation is to normalise the activity of its members and this is achieved not simply by the imposition of rules from above, but by the power which inheres in daily interactions and networks of relationships. Such power is not solely negative in the sense of being limiting or proscriptive.

Rather it is "actively directed towards the body and its possibilities, converting it into something both useful and docile" (Burrell, 1988). It is also not solely directed towards subordinates, for superordinates are also disciplined by the power of normalisation. The paradox of normalisation, however, is that it does not exclude difference. On the contrary, the very exercise of categorising serves to highlight difference, but in such a way that it does not threaten the organisation since difference can be accommodated within normality:

"In a sense, the power of normalisation imposes homogeneity; but it individualises by making it possible to measure gaps, to determine levels, to fix specialities and to render the differences useful by fitting them one to another." (Foucault, 1977:184)

The Probation Service has been largely impervious to such analyses and has accepted the rise of managerialism and the erosion of professional autonomy as an inevitable and to some extent desirable development. The emphasis on greater consistency of service delivery and greater accountability throughout the organisation's hierarchy has been welcomed by many and has been viewed as a pre-requisite for equality of opportunity at all levels of the service. The assumption underlying equal opportunity policies is that clarity (or articulacy) is essential and that anything which smacks of uncertainty, ambivalence or ambiguity (or mutedness) is likely to be discriminatory. Establishing clear expectations, boundaries and procedures is seen to safeguard the rights of all workers and reassure members of "minority" groups that their contributions are re valued and judged by fair and open criteria.

40

The irony should be apparent. The elevation of the formal in relation to equal opportunities serves only to buttress the formal character of the service as a whole and make it accessible only to those who are capable of functioning within that framework.

It is not just (and it is certainly not all) white women and black people who question the emphasis on the formal in the Probation Service. A small number of white male voices (including Humphrey, 1991; Humphrey and Pease, 1992) have sought to keep the management debate open. Perhaps the most persistent has been McWilliams (1992) who makes an important distinction between formal accountability and substantive accountability, arguing that it is disingenuous to claim that a management ethos is the only safeguard of standards. On the contrary, the proliferation of directives and procedures minimises the extent to which the organisation or any individual in it can be held accountable, especially if things go wrong. So long as the correct procedures are observed, no one can be blamed. Substantive accountability, on the other hand, requires an individual or group or organisation to give an account of its action. Undoubtedly, such accounts will be messy and confused and open to criticism, but it is only by engaging with the contradictions and paradoxes that characterise virtually any human transaction that we can ensure that all workers (and users) feel that they have been fairly treated.

CONCLUSION

In this chapter I have attempted to develop two main arguments. The first concerns the archaeology of the discourse of anti-discriminatory practice in social work generally and probation work specifically. In excavating the "values archive" of social work I have demonstrated a continuous concern with the interpretation and management of difference. I hope I have not, however, fallen into the trap of implying that the history of these ideas has been one of increasing coherence and unilinear progress. Instead, I have sought to show the fragmentary, partial and contradictory nature of the sets of statements which have been produced at various periods of social work's history and packaged as received wisdom. It has been my thesis that such incompleteness is inevitable and not undesirable. It is only when debate is foreclosed and a particular package of received wisdom is reified that tyranny creeps in, unrecognised until it is too late.

My second concern, which is closely linked with the first, has been to question the assumption that white women and black men and women working in the Probation Service will feel a greater sense of belonging to, and investment in, a Service which demonstrates greater commitment to formal equal opportunities policies and practices. I have not, for one minute, suggested that such policies should be neglected, but I have argued that there is an ironic danger that too much emphasis on a particular mode of communication, which I have termed "articulacy" may serve to render certain groups and individuals "muted" by reason of their inability to participate with a sufficient degree of clarity, confidence and "objectivity".

These two arguments are connected by a common concern that organisations have a tendency to normalise and homogenise - in relation both to service delivery and employment - in the name of accountability and quality assurance. In the present political climate, the Probation Service may feel that it has little option but to present a public image of a confident and well-disciplined workforce, meeting targets and objectives to a consistent and high standard. But it does not have to believe its own publicity. It may just be that genuine anti-discriminatory practice and equal opportunities can only be achieved by less, rather than more, formality and by a greater, rather than lesser, tolerance of heterogeneity - or difference.

[1]**No attempt is made here to define the difference between the terms "equal opportunities" and "anti-discriminatory practice" except to comment that the latter signifies a particular discourse within social work whereas the former represents an enterprise which social work has in common with all other employing organisations. The term "anti-oppressive practice" is not used at all because the writer feels that there is, as yet, no adequate definition of this particular distinction and that, in order to establish one, a separate discussion is required.**

[2]**The term "black" is used here in accordance with the definition employed by Dholakia & Sumner (1993):**
"Anyone who, whatever their nationality or culture, suffers from discrimination based on skin colour and is not accepted as 'white'. This does not imply that there is homogeneity in the experience of black people: in particular, the experiences which Asian and Afro-Caribbean people have of criminal justice are known to differ in important respects." **(Dholakia & Sumner, 1993:44)**

Unless otherwise stated, it has been accepted that the central concern of black women is "racial oppression and the gender specificity of racism" (Day, 1992). For this reason, discussion of black women is separated from discussion of white women, although it is accepted that this may not feel appropriate for some black women readers.

References

Allan, M., Bhavnani, R. & French, K. *Promoting Women*, Department of Health Social Services Inspectorate, HMSO, 1992

Ardener, S. *Defining Women*, Croom Helm, 1978

Bailey, R. & Brake, M. *Radical Social Work*, Edward Arnold, 1975

Biestek, F. *The Casework Relationship*, Allen Unwin, 1961

Bottoms, A. & McWilliams,W. "A non-treatment paradigm for probation practice", *British Journal of Social Work*,9(2), 159-202, 1979

Burrell, G. "Modernism, postmodernism and organizational analysis 2: the contribution of Michel Foucault", *Organization Studies*, 9(2), 1988, 221-235

Carlen, P. *Women's Imprisonment*, Routledge and Kegan Paul, 1983

Carlen, P. *et al Criminal Women*, Cambridge, Polity Press, 1985

Carlen, P. *Women, Crime and Poverty*, Milton Keynes, Open University Press, 1988

Carlen, P. *Alternatives to women's imprisonment*, Buckingham, Open University Press, 1990

Coleman, G. Investigating Organisations: a feminist approach, *Occasional Paper 37*, School for Advanced Urban Studies, University of Bristol, 1991

Cook, D. & Hudson, B. (eds) *Racism and Criminology*, Sage, 1993

Cooper, R. & Burrell, G. "Modernism, postmodernism and organizational analysis : an introduction", *Organization Studies,* 9(1), 1988, 91-112

Cordery, J. & Whitehead, A. "Boys don't cry: empathy, warmth, collusion and crime" in Senior, P. & Woodhill, D. (eds) *Gender, Crime and Probation Practice*, Sheffield, PAVIC Publications, 1992

Corrigan, P. & Leonard, P. *Social Work Practice under Capitalism*, Macmillan, 1978

Day, L. 'Women and oppression: race, class and gender" in Langan, M. & Day, L. (eds) *Women, Oppression and Social Work*, Routledge, 1992

Denney, D. *Racism and Anti-racism in Probation*, Routledge, 1992

Department of Health Social Services Inspectorate *Women in Social Services: a neglected resource*, HMSO, 1991

Eaton, M. *Justice for Women?*, Milton Keynes, Open University Press, 1986

Eaton, M. *Women after Prison*, Buckingham, Open University Press, 1993

Gilroy, P. *There ain't no black in the Union Jack*, Routledge, 1987

Haxby, D. *Probation: a Changing Service*, Constable, 1978

Hayles, M. "Promotion and Management: what choice for women?", *Probation Journal*, 36(1), 1989, 12-17

Heidensohn, F. Women and Crime, Macmillan, 1985

Home Office CJA section 95: *Race and the Criminal Justice System*, London, Home Office, 1992

Hudson, A. "Feminism and social work: resistance or dialogue?", *British Journal of Social Work*, 15, 1985, 635-655

Hudson, A. "Boys will be boys", *Critical Social Policy*, Spring, 1988, 30-48

Humphrey, C. "Calling on the Experts", *The Howard Journal of Criminal Justice*, 30(1), 1991, 1-18

Humphrey, C. & Pease, K. "Effectiveness measurement in the Probation Service: a view from the troops", *The Howard Journal of Criminal Justice*, 31(1), 1992, 31-52

Jones, C. "Distortion and demonisation: the right and anti-racist social work education", *Social Work Education*, 12(3) 1993, 9-16

Langan, M. & Day, L. (eds) *Women, Oppression and Social Work*, Routledge, 1992

McCaughey, C. "Making masculinity explicit in work with male offenders" in Senior, P. & Woodhill, D. (eds) *Gender, Crime and Probation Practice*, Sheffield, PAVIC Publications ,1992

McWilliams, W. "The rise and development of management thought in the English probation system" in Statham, R. & Whitehead, P. (eds) *Managing the Probation Service: issues for the 1990s*, Harlow, Longman, 1992

Matthews, R. & Young, J. (eds) *Confronting Crime*, Sage, 1986

Merchant, D. "Gender: a management perspective" in Senior, P. & Williams, B. (eds) *Values, Gender and Offending*, Sheffield, PAVIC Publications, 1993

NACRO *Black people working in the criminal justice system*, NACRO , 1992

Pitts, J. "Black young people and juvenile crime: some unanswered questions" in Matthews, R. & Young, J. (eds) *Confronting Crime*, Sage, 1986

Pitts, J. "Theorotyping: anti-racism, criminology and black young people" in Cook, D. & Hudson, B. (eds) *Racism and Criminology*, Sage, 1993

Rojek, C., Peacock, G. & Collins, S. *Social Work and Received Ideas*, Routledge, 1988

Senior, P. & Woodhill, D. (eds) *Gender, Crime and Probation Practice,* Sheffield, PAVIC Publications, 1992

Senior, P. & Williams, B. (eds) *Values, Gender and Offending,* Sheffield, PAVIC Publications , 1993

Smart, C. *Women, Crime and Criminology*, Routledge and Kegan Paul, 1976

Statham, R. & Whitehead, P. (eds) *Managing the Probation Service: issues for the 1990s*, Harlow, Longman, 1992

Walby, C. "Why are so few women working in senior positions?", *Social Work Today* 162, 1987, 10-11

Walker, H. & Beaumont, B. *Probation Work: Critical Theory and Socialist Practice,* Oxford, Basil Blackwell, 1981

Wells, O. *Promotion and the woman probation officer*, NAPO, 1983

Worrall, A. "The contribution to practice of gender perspectives in criminology" in Senior, P. & Williams, B. (eds) *Values, Gender and Offending*, Sheffield, PAVIC Publications, 1993

Worrall, A. "Gender, Criminal Justice and Probation Practice" in McIvor, G. (ed) Research Highlights in Social Work No 26, London, Jessica Kingsley, 1995

THREE: MANAGERIALISM AND THE PROBATION SERVICE

Bill Beaumont

This chapter considers developments in the management of the probation service since 1980, which I shall characterise as managerialism. These developments have been essentially politically driven, so attention is paid to the role of the Home Office in initiating and overseeing change. Events in the probation service closely parallel those in other public services and some attempt is made to sketch in this wider context. I chart three main strands in the way these government policies have been applied to, and within, the probation service;

* the application of "value for money" management practices
* the imposition of government "law and order" policy
* the application of pressure through the threat of privatisation

The chapter draws on my experience of these developments as a trade union representative for probation staff and provides a critical analysis from that perspective. It concludes by considering the current state of managerialism in the service and prospects for the future.

THE ARRIVAL OF MANAGEMENT

McWilliams (1992) has argued that the concept of management is a relatively recent arrival in the probation service. Other accounts of the service's organisational development (King, 1969; Bochel, 1976; Haxby, 1978; May, 1991) provide ample evidence to support that view. As late as 1972, the service's practice of "casework supervision" was described as closer to the academic than industrial sense of the word "supervision", and the service's view of management was said to be;

"largely ... an extension of supervision [and] ... an enabling function providing facilities for the main grade officers to perform their work satisfactorily"
(Butterworth Report cited in McWilliams, 1992: 11)

McWilliams (1992) has argued that till then the probation service had operated, satisfactorily, a professional-administrative model of

47

organisation. However, the Butterworth Report (1972), in claiming that there was an increasing need for planning and control, heralded the management era.

McWilliams (1992) identifies several factors which contributed to the shift to a management model - increased size and complexity in staffing and organisation; increasing range of functions; increasing emphasis on national policy and planning; importation of ideas about "modern management techniques" from the Prison Service; and the profound impact of the "nothing works"analysis (Martinson, 1974; Brody, 1976). Others have suggested additional factors - the shift in formal responsibility introduced by parole (Haxby,1978); pressure from probation officers for improved organisation and supervision (especially during the "casework" era), and for improved promotion prospects (Bochel, 1976; Haxby, 1978; May, 1991).

The development of a bureaucratic hierarchy and then, from the seventies, a management structure was frequently the focus of conflict in the service. The Butterworth Report (1972), which endorsed a more managerial approach, also slipped its new managers a time bomb - an early version of performance -related pay required senior staff to decide which officers' performance merited the higher B grade. The seventies saw not only the growth of management in the service but a period of intense conflict between probation officers and senior staff. Some probation officers, through the National Association of Probation Officers (NAPO), questioned the developing management structure and argued for seniorless teams. Another factor influencing the development of a management approach was the development of trade union consciousness amongst staff.

To help settle this unrest, the Joint Negotiating Committee (JNC) agreed to establish a Working Party on Management Structure. Not surprisingly, its main report dismissed criticisms of the emerging management structure. It provides a convenient statement of how probation management was seen as we enter the period on which this chapter now focuses:

> *". . . . it is no longer sufficient to look upon management . . . . as purely a means of enabling probation officers to practise their social work skills . . . . Its primary task is to identify the tasks which society requires of the service, and to develop ways of discharging these responsibilities most effectively . . . . the functions of management appear to be sixfold;*

(a) to formulate policy and to set objectives

(b) to organise the undertaking by identifying the activities necessary to achieve the objectives

(c) to classify the work so that it may be divided and assigned to individuals and groups

(d) to motivate staff to make their contribution for the purposes of the organisation

(e) to provide supervision, support and training

(f) to measure actual performance against the original plan"   (JNC, 1980, 19)

Less than a decade on, the Working Party had chosen to ignore the Butterworth Report's (1972) warning that selecting "the right style of management for social services is not easy" (72) and had endorsed a reasonably straightforward, and even at that time rather dated, management style. In little over a decade, the probation service had moved from a professional-administrative model of organisation to face the challenges of the eighties from the fragile base of a newly-achieved and unsophisticated management model.

THE CENTRAL IMPERATIVE

Despite the formal status of probation as a local service, central government has always played a significant role in its affairs. The power of the Home Office, as a major funder of the service, is apparant but until recently its use was mediated by the Byzantine conventions that existed in relations between central and local government. The Home Office's concern to influence the probation service's work was heightened with what McWilliams (1992) describes as the "rise of policy" from the sixties onwards. May (1991) argues that central government concerns in this period became fourfold - public anxiety about rising crime; the increasing prison population; the high cost of imprisonment (especially providing more prisons); and the consequent search for alternatives to custody. These led the Home Office to press the probation service to develop new "alternatives to custody" which to be credible with the courts, it was argued, had to involve more controlling approaches. May (1991) suggests that the probation service had become "wedged between central government concerns and the sentencing decisions of judges and magistrates" (20). Already, as it entered the eighties, the new probation management structure was under pressure to deliver centrally generated policy objectives.

It is important to note that the term "central government", as it is used here, consists of two elements - the government itself, in the form of Ministers, and the executive, their professional Civil Service. What is described above as a set of "central government concerns" spanned Conservative and Labour governments and owed much to a continuity of Civil Service concerns. However, the Conservative government elected in 1979 not only had a distinctive and radical policy line on many issues but had also diagnosed public service bureaucrats, including Civil Servants, as part of the problem they intended to tackle. Three radical right policy themes have particular significance for this discussion - the promise to re-establish "law and order"; the effort to dismantle as much as politically possible of the welfare state; and a determined effort to change radically the management culture of the public sector. It is important to note that these policies have been commonplace internationally.

The apparently relentless rise in recorded crime in the "liberal democracies" has continued to drive a search for new law and order strategies in the United States, Europe, Australia and New Zealand. There are many similarities in the approaches tried - increased use of imprisonment, a search for cheaper but tough alternatives to custody, experimentation with the privatisation of prisons and interest in the use of electronic surveillance. Culpitt (1992) records that "fundamental changes to the political structure of the welfare state have been made with very little debate" in New Zealand and argues that, internationally, neo-conservative critics have succeeded in "pre-empting any debate about the role of the state other than its reduction"(2). One strand that uncomfortably unites neo-conservative and radical critics of the welfare state is concern about the unresponsive bureaucracies they spawned. Neo-conservatives focus on the economic consequences and blame the managers. Culpitt (1992) summarises their argument thus:

> *"because there are no economic or external incentives for*
> *effective management, public sector bureaucrats inevitably*
> *become inherent 'empire-builders' who seek only to enlarge*
> *the size and scope of their organisation"* (8).

Consequently public sector management is seen as a key target for radical transformation. In their study of how this has affected the courts in England and Wales, Raine and Willson (1993) cite Hood who characterises the outcome as the New Public Management (NPM), an international trend in public administration. Hood (1991) identifies seven doctrines of NPM:

* hands-on professional management
* explicit standards and measures of performance
* greater emphasis on output controls (a focus on results not procedures)
* shift to disaggregation of units in the public sector
* shift to more competition in the public sector
* stress on private-sector styles of management practice
* stress on greater discipline and parsimony in resource use.

Returning to the specific British context, in 1979 one of the first targets for transformation was the Civil Service itself. The Cabinet Office Efficiency Unit was established, under Sir Derek Rayner, to improve efficiency and eliminate waste in government departments. By 1982, this early work led to publication of the government's Financial Management Initiative, which each government department was enjoined to pursue in each area of activity:

- economy, efficiency and effectiveness (the three Es)
- a critical questioning of the role of the public sector
- changing management practices to improve performance
- greater accountability, cash limits and value for money
- the setting of objectives, priorities and targets.

(Whitehead, 1992)

Before turning to examine how this broad government strategy has been applied to the probation service, it is necessary to note that the agenda is essentially ideological and the solutions doctrinal. "Value for money" (VfM) is inevitably a subjective judgement - huge waste is tolerable on projects which the government favours while services which it dislikes will find it impossible to prove they give "VfM". In the three Es the greatest of the three is always economy - efficiency is usually constructed as the cheapest option even if the outcome is demonstrably poorer and there is singularly little interest in achieving effectiveness. The answer to critical questioning of the role of the public sector is dogmatically fixed in advance - the acceptable answer always has to be a reduced role (even if the process of achieving it seems exceptionally costly!). The central imperative for all public sector managers is to implement government policy.

51

DANCING TO ANOTHER'S TUNE

Although the Home Office has always influenced probation service developments, since 1980 this influence has reached unprecedented heights. Put crudely, as it was by some Civil Servants in the course of discussions, he (or she) who pays the piper, calls the tune. There have been variations in the central imperative issuing from government - from the early uncertainty of the Whitelaw years, through Patten's "window of opportunity", to the crude certainty of Michael Howard's "prison works" - but in recent years there can be little doubt that the:

"onslaught of initiatives and directions has not so much influenced but rather driven management thinking and processes".

(Statham, 1992, 39)

It is in this process that management in the probation service has come to exhibit, with varying degrees of enthusiasm, all the characteristics of NPM. I now trace this development in relation to three main themes - VfM Management, law and order policy and privatisation.

"VALUE FOR MONEY" MANAGEMENT

The probation service largely escaped the efficiency scrutinies and cuts experienced by parts of the public sector in the Conservatives' first term. Even initial application of the Financial Management Initiative (FMI) was gradual. The first rumbles, in the early eighties, took the form of a newly critical Home Office attitude towards probation service management. This, of course, makes sense in terms of the "new right" analysis which targeted public sector managers but came as a considerable shock to Chief Probation Officers (CPOs). They found themselves being told they had to learn to manage. Humphrey (1991), an accountancy lecturer, used the experience of the probation service as a case study in the application of FMI. He noted that the broad logic dictated two distinct phases of development:

- specification of national and local statements of objectives and priorities
- creation of a financial management information system to assist in monitoring performance against those objectives and priorities.

I will now look at these two separate but interrelated strands in turn.

MANAGEMENT BY OBJECTIVES

The first step in developing management by objectives (MBO) was for the Home Office to model it in formulating their Statement of National Objectives and Priorities (SNOP). It was immediately clear that priorities were to be set by rationing resources between existing activities, rather than prioritising desirable improvements. Although there was a consultation process involving ACOP (Association of Chief Officers of Probation, the managers), CCPC (Central Council of Probation Committees, the employers) and NAPO (the staff), it marked the beginning of an era of "minimalist consultation". All parties were clear that the outcome was predetermined by government policy. Increasingly, the timescale would be so shortened as to make even "minimalist consultation" tokenistic.

The SNOP consultation was one forum in which Home Office officials pressed their new "systems model" of criminal justice agencies. For the Home Office, whose responsibilities span four services - the police, courts, prisons, and probation - it is easy to see the attractions of a "systems" approach. From almost any other perspective the doubts about whether a "criminal justice system" actually exists command more weight. However, the;

> *"greatest tribute to an idea is to acknowledge that it has moulded one's thinking and has become the dominant paradigm outside of which it is hard to imagine."*

(Raine and Willson, 1993: 61)

The "criminal justice system" has indeed become the dominant paradigm in probation discourse since 1984. SNOP also marked a language shift - the people with whom the service worked were no longer clients (never a satisfactory term) but uniformly offenders, a term which denies their existence as complex human beings capable of a wide range of behaviour.

SNOP (Home Office,1984a), when published, firmly reflected the government's organisational and penal policy imperatives. Both the choice of priorities, and the language in which they were expressed, reflected the government's intention to shift the orientation of the probation service towards correctionalism. Although, in retrospect, mild compared with what would follow, SNOP was identified at the time as seeking "to minimise the social work role of the probation service" (Walker and Beaumont, 1985: 12). The statement was coolly received by probation committees, managers and staff (NAPO,1984) alike. Following SNOP, services were expected to develop statements of local objectives and priorities (rather graphically known as SLOPs). These were analysed by Lloyd

(1986) who concluded their most notable feature was "diversity" and that:

> *"conflicts between Home Office/Government and Service principles seem to underlie most of the disagreements between SNOP and local areas"* (cited in May, 1991,43).

The immediate impact of SNOP (and SLOPs) was probably disappointing to the Home Office, confirming that more direct pressure was required, but it did start a culture shift within probation management.

SNOP was not an isolated initiative. The newly amended Probation Rules defined the CPO as "responsible for the direction of the probation service in his [sic] area, for its effective operation and the efficient use of its resources" (Home Office, 1984b). The importance of VfM and MBO was repeatedly emphasised to probation managers:

> *"the basic management by objectives approach was reinforced by the Home Office's promotion of Gilpin Black and other firms of management consultants. Effectiveness seminars were provided by the Home Office for senior managers, who were then encouraged to buy-in their expertise as part of a process of developing an in-house management culture".*

> (Statham, 1992, 40)

Over the next couple of years most area management teams underwent MBO training. The areas which adopted the style most enthusiastically soon had each probation team setting precise objectives to be achieved the following year. This process, in one county, is analysed in depth by May (1991) who points both to the arbitrariness of some objective-setting and the deep alienation engendered. Parry-Khan (1988) suggested, "inefficiency and wastage of energy have not been dispelled by MBO - they have flourished"(33).

By 1988 the Home Office was confident enough of its authority over local probation services to set them a compulsory practical exercise in MBO. Following publication of the Green Paper "Punishment, Custody and the Community" (Home Office, 1988a), each probation service was required to produce an Action Plan for tackling offending by young adults and submit it "to the Home Office for scrutiny" (Statham, 1992: 42). Probation service managements, scared by the Green Paper's threats of privatisation and marginalisation, complied. Civil servants hinted that the outcome might influence the government's thinking about the need to adopt the more radical Green Paper proposals. There was little evidence that the content of Action Plans had any effect on government policy. Harman (1990) notes:

> *"I and others put a large amount of work into producing the Action Plan, It was not acknowledged by the Home Office. It was not clear how the Home Office evaluated Action Plans . . ."* (17)

This disregard of outcomes is not, of course, consistent with modelling good MBO practice but by this time, Home Office Civil Servants (under government pressure) seemed more interested in simple obedience training.

By the time of the next Green Paper, "Supervision and Punishment in the Community" (Home Office,1990b), the focus was shifting to other elements of government policy - change by legislation, threats of radical reorganisation, pressure from privatisation, central direction by national standards - but the pursuit of improved management continued and MBO was the underlying management model. By the early nineties, the second strand of FMI (cost-consciousness via financial management information systems) had developed considerably and the two strands were increasingly interlinked in operation, leading Kemshall (1993a) to suggest that a new phase, of Finance and Resource Management, had been entered.

The growth of MBO over 10 years had not been without its critics amongst probation management. Concern was expressed that MBO was contrary to social work values and the principles of a learning organisation (Vanstone and Seymour,1986); was placing conflicting demands on seniors (Boswell,1986); was leading to a "macho management ethos"(Thomas and Vanstone, 1992); and was an old-fashioned management style which had been abandoned by businesses (Lewis,1991; Shaw, 1992). Kemshall (1993a) concluded that:

> *"MBO in its present form has led managers increasingly into a monitoring and control function, with top-down imposition of objectives and managers at the middle level increasingly enmeshed in administrative and bureaucratic systems to scrutinise what staff do."* (6)

FMIS - The Rise of Accountancy

The second strand in applying FMI, development of a Financial Management Information System (FMIS), represents the rise of accountancy in the affairs of the probation service. The first task in developing FMIS was to devise some performance measures. Humphrey (1991) records that the Inspectorate "fell down at their first hurdle - the recording of what probation staff did"(4). By 1985, Ministers had stepped in, cancelled the planned work and ordered civil servants to engage management consultants. Deloitte, Haskins and Sells (DHS) were appointed and Humphrey (1991) records Home Office optimism that private sector experts would solve a problem created by a "lack of financial expertise within the Service" rather than "any inherent limitations of the logic of the FMI" (6). It was soon obvious, however, that the consultants were also in deep difficulty, including the problem on which the Inspectorate foundered - measuring use of staff time. In September 1987, they reported that their system would cost another £5-10 million and take four more years to develop. In a face-saving formula, work on FMIS continued under direct Home Office control with DHS relegated to an advisory role.

The FMIS project had thus far made no contribution to service effectiveness. Had the project, and the involvement of the consultants, proved cost-effective? Strangely enough, this does not appear to be a question which is askable! Humphrey (1991) cites the National Audit Office as surprisingly prepared to accept that the cost-effectiveness of FMIS cannot be measured and concludes"

"In a world where value-for-money is apparently king, it is difficult . . . to think of approval being given to any service related plans on the scale of FMI . . . solely on the grounds that they are worth doing, even though their effects cannot be measured." (15)

The push for cost-conscious management continued undeterred. A Rayner-style efficiency scrutiny (Home Office,1987) confined the Probation Inspectorate to a narrow concern with the three Es, presumably as the cost of fluffing early work on FMIS. In 1988/89 the probation service experienced an accounting "double whammy" - simultaneous studies by the Audit Commission, of local services, and the National Audit Office (1989), of Home Office performance. Both reports are curiously dated documents - they seek to build on a government approach now abandoned. They reflect a weakness in the ability of accountants to assess effectiveness - the Audit Commission report indicates a fair beginner's grasp of complex and under-researched issues (such as the impact of probation supervision and the displacement effects of alternatives to custody) but in the end had to settle for the fashionable wisdom of the moment.

Since such exercises can add little to existing debates on effectiveness, it is engaging that the Audit Commission was so frank about its main role saying that in "current circumstances it is hard to assess the value for money provided by the probation service" (Audit Commission, 1989, 3).

Pressure on probation service management to become cost-conscious was also coming from local authorities which, under pressure from central government, were introducing new budgeting systems. Increasingly smaller units were being identified as "cost-centres" including, in some areas, individual offices. Kemshall (1993a), in an article entitled "Are We All Accountants Now?", warns that managers may:

"become imprisoned by the data, unwilling to make decisions under any situation of uncertainty, managing work against performance indicators and outcomes limited in their original conception" (6).

The local pressures continued with each probation service audited during 1990/91 - the Audit Commission's report (1991) of these local audits interestingly stressed the need for wider application of simple approaches, rather than the development of more complex management systems.

Despite this accountant's plea for simplicity, work on FMIS continued, now transformed into the Resource Management Information System (RMIS). Whitehead (1992) has reported on the close links between attempts to develop these information systems and the service's growing expenditure on computers, another area in which VfM criteria appear to be ignored. Bowyer (1992) reported that RMIS was to be introduced in eight probation areas for a short pilot run before full implemention in 1992/93. He summarised NAPO's basic concerns thus:

"issues of cost and quantity will override issues of quality and . . . efficiency will become all important at the expense of effectiveness" (Bowyer, 1992, 10)

Eschewing complexity, the Home Office had meanwhile put the probation service on notice that it intended to introduce cash limits. Despite all the development work of the eighties the government decided it still could not tell which services were working, by Home Office standards, efficiently or effectively and opted instead to distribute grant by formula. Economy had triumphed again.

LAW AND ORDER POLICY

In the early eighties there was broad consensus between managers and staff on some issues - shared concern about the direction of government social policy and especially its effect on young people; about punitive innovations like "short, sharp shock" regimes and restrictions on parole; to see appropriate probation service intervention increased and reliance on imprisonment decreased. The differences were, not surprisingly, greatest on issues closest to probation practice. Some CPOs favoured development of more intensive supervision schemes - for example, the Kent Control Unit and tracking schemes. ACOP worked with the Home Office to overcome, in the Criminal Justice Act 1982, the brake put on intensive day centre programmes by an adverse legal judgment. The introduction of the curfew as a condition of supervision orders demarcated one crucial difference between CPOs and their staff. NAPO members, largely successfully, boycotted the curfew and other "restrictive" conditions, preventing their use. Most CPOs did not welcome the curfew provision but saw it as their duty to implement the government policy. The grounds for tensions to come were already laid.

Anticipating a radical policy initiative on "law and order", the three main probation organisations decided to greet the third Conservative government with a united front. They produced a joint statement which argued that developments should:

> *"build upon the established strengths of the probation service, utilise the skills of its professional and other fieldwork staff and work with the grain of the service. Any other approach risks disorientation, dislocations and inefficiency"* (ACOP/CCPC/NAPO,1987, 3).

It was quickly clear that there was little prospect of deflecting the whirlwind of change to come. Opinion began to divide sharply within ACOP and a "new realist" position started to gain sway. This did not represent ideological congruence with the government but held that major change had to be accepted as the price for survival. The positions of NAPO and ACOP diverged rapidly; ironically NAPO and CCPC (the employers' organisation) stayed generally closer in their opposition to the changes to come. The management of the service was to prove most flexible in seeking to accommodate the new central imperative - punishment in the community.

Government thinking was trailed extensively before publication of the Green Paper (Home Office,1988a). Consultations on National Standards for Community Service Orders made it clear that Civil Servants were now working to a very tight ministerial brief. Some senior managers were beginning to convince themselves that the service had always been in the "punishment" business. An ACOP sub-committee produced a discussion paper "More Demanding Than Prison" (ACOP, 1988). In an attempt to provide 'creative and flexible leadership', it proposed a new community restitution order combining community service, training in a day centre and residential restrictions (to include curfews). ACOP's pre-emptive strike turned out to be more punitive than the Green Paper's proposed new order and its members eventually rejected both proposals.

The Green Paper's "punishment in the community" theme was a compromise between the government's push to get tough and civil servants' concerns about the prison population. David Faulkner clearly saw this compromise policy as a reasonable outcome from difficult negotiations with ministers. He had lobbied assiduously amongst penal reformers and, for such a reactionary document, the Green Paper got a curiously mixed reception from the penal reform lobby (see Rees and Hall Williams, 1989; Shaw and Haines, 1989). On behalf of ACOP, Smith (1989) welcomed the Green Paper as heralding an "intention to effect an element of radical change in the criminal justice system" (p112) while registering their opposition to the proposed "supervision and restriction order". The Home Office pressed on with its Action Plans initiative and the final version of National Standards for Community Service. Tension in the service remained high and affected managers:

"the constant barrage of policy and practice requirements from the Home Office leaves managers feeling potentially despondent about their own previous practice" (Harman, 1990, 16).

The central government onslaught continued. The White Paper, "Crime, Justice and Protecting the Public" (Home Office,1990a) embraced both punishment in the community and changes to release provisions for prisoners, based on the Carlisle Committee Report (Home Office,1988c). Although the government had edged away from introducing a new order all the main elements of the punishment in the community theme were still there. The new release proposals for prisoners were intended to close, and render more predictable, the gap between sentence imposed and time served. The White Paper made bold claims for these proposals - they would provide "a new and more coherent framework for sentencing" (Home Office, 1990a). On the journey between Green and White Papers, Home Office Civil Servants had found a unifying theme - "just deserts". They had also managed to persuade ministers to attempt a radical shift in sentencers' thinking - to focus attention on the seriousness of the offence before them, rather than the offender's criminal record. This had not been widely discussed or well prepared, and was in time to prove the undoing of the entire strategy.

The Green Paper (Home Office,1990b), which accompanied the White Paper, was intended to keep the pressure on the probation service. It examined options for reorganisation, including amalgamating smaller services; greater use of Home Office powers to enforce change; moving to 100 per cent central government funding; moving to a national service under direct Home Office control or as a separate agency; and, of course, various forms of contracting with the voluntary or private sectors. Given the power the Home Office was already wielding, these proposals were clearly intended to secure, and proved effective in securing, even more compliance from management with the central thrust of government policy. Once the Criminal Justice Bill was under way, and the service was deemed to be reacting appropriately, the Home Office produced its follow up Decision Document (Home Office, 1991a) making only minor changes to the structure of the service. The frighteners were off for the moment.

The Home Office decided that successful implementation of the Criminal Justice Act 1991 depended heavily on the work of the probation service in courts and the service, still reeling from a ferocious rubbishing from the Home Office, suddenly found itself subject to a charm offensive. Resources were to be provided for the extra work coming its way. Consultations on the National Standards changed in tone and the service organisations briefly felt they were being listened to again on some issues. However, Home Office control was further demonstrated when it deemed that all probation officers should receive training on the Act and services should spend all their 1992/93 training budgets on it. NACRO was commissioned to provide some very elaborate training materials and probation staff were released for three to five days' training prior to implementation. The Home Office finalised its National Standards document - for once each probation officer received a copy of a Home Office document. Given the fate of the 1991 Act, a VfM analysis of this implementation programme might make interesting reading.

How then was probation management reacting to government "law and order" policy? May (1991) suggests:

"Probation management ... are increasingly criticised by probation officers for the lack of any social work input into policy initiatives. It appears that they are reacting to Home Office directives ...."(34)

Managers varied in their attitude to these directives. Some were early converts to the new equation - probation equals punishment - but the majority view in ACOP rejected the new orders proposed from within their own ranks and by the 1988 Green Paper. The "new realists" toyed with taking on tagging, but the majority were opposed and the government turned to the private sector for its experimentation. However, the majority within ACOP came to accept that "punishment in the community"could be looked on as an issue of semantics, and that the 1991 Act was a progressive measure offering the probation service a more central role in the criminal justice system. One CPO, Statham (1992) argued:

"even where there may be a negative perception of national standards and punishment in the community, there is an equally valid alternative view. Promoting the alternative view, when there are also feelings about being over-managed following the national standards initiatives, will not be easy". (74)

In the event, the probation service's moment centre stage was indeed short-lived, as the government's enchantment with its own creation proved remarkably fragile. Even as courts and probation officers struggled to make sense of the 1991 Act's convoluted provisions on "seriousness" and "mitigating and aggravating factors", government ministers were preparing to disown the work of their predecessors. The 1993 Criminal Justice Act unpicked key provisions and Michael Howard's arrival at the Home Office signalled a new central imperative on penal policy. Now it seems "prison works" and is cast as the safe alternative to community penalties. The probation service is still required to deliver "punishment in the community" but now as an adjunct to, rather than a replacement for, the central role of imprisonment. Many probation managers, who had accepted a punishment role in exchange for a centre stage location, are now deeply disillusioned by the disintegration of that dream. The government continues to call the tune, but no one is dancing with enthusiasm to the new one.

PRIVATISATION

The threat of privatisation has been a crucial element in the government's policies towards the public services and its effect on probation service developments is far from negligible. Ryan and Ward (1991) have suggested that the government's purpose has been:

"not mainly to secure greater consistency or a more cost-effective service, but primarily to coerce the probation service into delivering tougher alternatives to custody". (54)

In the run-up to SNOP, Home Office officials leaked news of high-level discussions which contemplated the break-up of the probation service and, at least, partial privatisation. This threat became a recurrent theme in the years to follow and operated to lessen resistance, from within the service, to unwelcome changes. This paralleled a similar use of the threat across all criminal justice agencies.

Only after 1987 did a serious intent to privatise begin to take shape; Douglas Hurd "moved from dismissing the idea of privatisation of prisons as unacceptable, to announcing he had no objection in principle to a private company running a remand centre" (Lilley and Knepper,1992: 181). The 1988 Green Paper on "Private Sector Involvement in the Remand System" (Home Office, 1988b) included interest in the development of what were termed "secure bail hostels". The private sector interests which had lobbied for a change of government policy on prisons were also interested in such hybrid developments.

Privatisation seemed at first an empty threat to most in the probation service. As Drakeford (1988) noted, the

"important core of probation activity . . . involves messy and difficult face-to-face work with individuals living at the nexus of multiple disadvantage and popular disapproval. There is no simple profit to be extracted from such encounters . . ." (44)

However, the government was progressively developing a range of approaches to overcome the fact that not all public services were attractive to the private sector. Beaumont (1987) pointed out that voluntary organisations active in work with offenders were potentially the main vehicle for privatisation initiatives. The threat of privatisation was given concrete form in the 1988 Green Paper and the Audit Commission (1989) perceived it clearly:

"The probation service is therefore at a critical point. It can either move to the forefront of the government's penal policy; or it could find that another agency is given responsibility for new community options and, perhaps, part of its existing workload." (6)

The Home Office invited voluntary organisations to bid for new funds for work with young adult offenders. NAPO's response to the Green Paper indicated concern that privatisation could allow the government to side-step opposition to punishment in the community (NAPO,1988). The ACOP response is described by Ryan and Ward (1991) as:

> *"a rather bland 'Position Statement' which viewed the voluntary and private sectors as a 'huge pool of resources and potential support' and [suggested] that its members should take the initiative in developing and co-ordinating inter-agency work".* (60)

A key concern of probation service managers was to ensure that they retained a central position in the contracting process.

In this context, considerable tension developed between probation service staff and the voluntary organisations bidding to develop young adult offender services. NAPO had traditionally lobbied for penal reform alongside the campaigning wings of the voluntary organisations involved. There was more common ideological ground between probation staff and voluntary sector employees than there was between either group and the government, or often between probation staff and their own management. But there was no mistaking the sudden rather predatory interest of voluntary agency managements in young adult offenders or the encouragement given to that interest by the Home Office. In an attempt to find a positive way through the conflict engendered by government policy, NAPO and six leading national voluntary organisations (Children's Society, CSV, NACRO, NCH, Rainer and Save the Children) produced a "Framework for Partnership" (NAPO *et al,*1990). This identified the appropriate role for voluntary organisations as "services and projects which complement the work of the probation service"(3).

The 1990 Green Paper bluntly spelt out the government's belief that;

> *"the disciplines of the market place can often serve as an effective guarantee of quality and value for money in the provision of public services".* (Home Office,1990b: 37)

The threat of a new agency had been dropped but the government wanted thorough exploration of the potential for "partnerships" between the probation service and what was termed the "independent sector". These issues were seen as sufficiently important to justify a separate Discussion Paper (Home Office,1990c).

Commentators (Nellis, 1990; Ryan and Ward,1991) have pointed to the tortuous terminology involved in government rhetoric. Voluntary sector voices (Errington, 1990; Kay, 1992) took strong exception to being bracketed together with commercial organisations. It is a moot point whether "voluntary organisations" are either voluntary or independent any longer. As Nellis (1990) points out:

> *"To the extent that the so-called voluntary sector is dependent for its existence on state funding - and large numbers of 'voluntary organisations' are - it is not a voluntary sector at all, and certainly not an independent sector. It is, in one sense, an arm of the state ..."* (38)

A shift in state support, unpopular with voluntary agencies, from "core funding" to "grant-aid" for specific projects has increased the centre's ability to control their activities. With the development of the contract culture, government can invite bids to run projects and determine their content in detail. As if to confirm its growing interdependency with the state, the voluntary sector has itself been subject to a government efficiency scrutiny (Efficiency Unit, 1990) which raised some doubts about whether this government expenditure achieved value for money!

The voluntary sector's misgivings about the government's "partnership" proposals were to emerge from the four consultation meetings which were supposed to take the initiative forward. Anxieties were expressed about the spread of the 'contract culture' which forces voluntary organisations to bid against each other; continued reliance on short-term funding which produces uncertainty an inefficiency; and the probation service's lead role in funding which compromised the equality needed for genuine "partnerships" (Stern, 1990; Errington, 1990). Other commentators (Fielder, 1991; Sarkis, 1993) have pointed out that the larger national voluntary organisations have the management structure and expertise to compete in the "contract culture" while local community organisations are likely to lose out.

Although the voluntary sector provides the main potential for the 'market place' the government seeks, attempts were made to involve the private sector in the four "partnerships" initiative consultations. At one, an American management consultant ascribed his presence to the fact that "there are very few private operators in the field in the United Kingdom" (Lovett, 1990). One such, Sir Edward Gardner QC, had attended the first consultation representing Bail Accommodation Ltd which he said "was concerned with the provision of bail hostels" (Gardner, 1990). The role of the Home Affairs Select Committee, on which Gardner served, in securing government support for the privatisation of prisons has been noted by Lilly and Knepper (1992). They also suggest that there is now an "international corrections market" and a "corrections-commercial" complex in the United States which "operates without public scrutiny and exercises enormous influence over corrections policy" (1975). The flow of influence and personnel which they identify as significant in that "corrections-commercial" complex has perhaps begun to develop here as well.

The government has started to create the conditions for a criminal justice market place. Three private remand prisons have been established and more are planned. Escorts to courts have been privatised in a trial scheme and gentle probes conducted into potential areas of privatisation in the highly sensitive area of policing. In relation to the probation service, however, Ryan and Ward's (1991) hypothesis that the main function (to date) of privatisation talk has been to coerce the service into compliance was supported by the Decision Document on the "partnership" initiative (Home Office 1991b). It proposed a relatively modest start, with probation services required to spend 5 per cent of their budgets on "partnership schemes" from 1993/4. The immediate impact on local services was limited because that 5 per cent was to include existing arrangements and some funds transferred from Home Office budgets.

Throughout these discussions probation management has focused its efforts on securing a central role in the new arrangements. Like voluntary sector managers, they have been encouraged to adopt a more entrepreneurial stance and it is attractive, in this context, to have secured grant-aiding powers. These significantly extend the range of managers' activities - service specification, deciding between tenders, negotiating contracts and contract enforcement. Matthews (1990) commented on the irony that at a time when the service's practitioners are being told to restrict themselves to core tasks, service managers are:

"being encouraged to engage in various administrative and managerial practices in which they have little or no experience". (55)

The new arrangements give probation service managers new powers - within the service, they can opt to spend money on developing the work of their own staff or on purchasing services from other organisations; within the local community, they become purchasers to be wooed by voluntary organisations. It is another role which sets managers apart from other probation staff.

THE ARRIVAL OF MANAGERIALISM

The cumulative effect of these developments has driven managers in the probation service beyond rational management models into managerialism. This has not been a comfortable transition for the managers. Raine and Willson (1993) graphically describe the process within the court system:

> *"the imposition of the new managerialism must have felt a little like being given school detention. In their own classrooms, and under the personal and critical-eyed supervision of the head-teacher, they were taught how to behave and to do as they were told . . . . there was a certain amount of shouting from the head and quite a few threats were issued as well. The class was made to recite out loud 'I must give priority to economy, efficiency and effectiveness' . . . 'I must be accountable for my actions', 'I must be more strategic in my approach', and 'I must do as the head-teacher tells me'".*(214)

For the probation service, detention was even more severe - the lines to be learnt also included "I must agree that probation can be a punishment" and "I must learn that my knowledge about offenders counts for nothing".

If the process has been uncomfortable for the managers it has been largely incomprehensible to the managed. The journalist Katherine Whitehorn (1993) caught this mood admirably when she wrote:

> *"I don't know a single charity or college or clinic, that once spent its time trying to reach more people or care more or teach better, that doesn't now spend half its time worrying about money"*

and suggesting, given the power of an apt phrase to discredit, that

> *what we need now is a word for the men in suits who think that everything comes down to profit and the bottom line."*

Two weeks later she reported being inundated with suggestions, including "cost-defectives", "ledger louts", and "Peevon" (for the man who, in Oscar Wilde's words, knows "the Price of Everything and the Value of Nothing").

I find "cost-defective" very expressive - it implies not only that the value placed on cost issues is defectively excessive but that the claim to epitomise cost-effectiveness is also seriously defective. The war on waste proves merely to be a preference for different forms of waste - some outcomes which might be considered highly desirable are arbitrarily classed as wasteful and ideologically-based preferences are portrayed as technical solutions no matter how wasteful they may be.

The key features of this era of managerialism in the probation service seem to be:

* acceptance that policy and objectives are set by central government and the duty of management is merely to carry out policy
* abandonment of the expectation that the professional experience of the probation service will have any effect on policy formation
* acceptance that a main role of management is to monitor adherence to detailed standards set by central government
* preoccupation with the process of management as opposed to the process of work with offenders
* preference for change-oriented activities at the expense of maintenance-oriented activities in the organisation
* acceptance that top-down management is a cost-effective way of operating all services
* acceptance that a narrow cost-consciousness is a key requirement for managers
* substitution of short-term targets for long-term goals
* preoccupation with the technology of management information systems, whatever their cost
* attachment of higher value to management activity than to the activities of front-line workers
* acceptance that the role of managers is to discipline front-line workers to perform closely specified tasks
* acceptance that the work of probation staff can be so routinised as to lend itself to detailed regulation.

THE FUTURE OF MANAGERIALISM

There is, as yet, little sign of any let up in the central imperative which has driven probation managers towards this form of managerialism. Some managers have used the ambiguity created by the "Citizen's Charter" to shift the focus of management training from "Management by Objectives" to "Total Quality Management". The same management consultants, Gilpin Black, who offered many services have started a second round of TQM training - a management consultant's work is never done. Kemshall (1993b) warns that an:

"emphasis on control, scrutiny and quality as a checking mechanism may only serve to reinforce the managerial attitude

that performance is enhanced by issuing prescriptive rules and standards, and that the main managerial objective is to seek strict adherence to them"(123).

Pursuing the search for ever more detailed prescription, the Home Office has published sets of competencies for main-grade and senior probation staff, against which it wants performance appraised. In a further exercise of centralised power, the Home Office has imposed a new appraisal system on services. In the JNC, the Home Office has insisted on performance-related pay for CPOs and ACPOs and is now intent on introducing a salary spine for all other staff which will lend itself to performance-related pay. Another element of the New Public Management style is about to be put in place.

One claim frequently made by probation managers throughout the last ten years, and by civil servants managing the government's plans, is that the changes required will put the service's house in order and protect it against further government criticism. As if to put a lie to that claim, John Major has declared the government's intention to publish a new Green Paper to:

"set new standards to ensure that probation and community service orders are 'tough and demanding'" (Guardian, 10th September 1994)

Does that sound familiar? It is surely now clear that a tougher probation service will not displace custody as the central punishment; instead the "coercive tilt is likely to produce a harder probation service, servicing a harsher penal system" (Walker and Beaumont, 1981; 152).

There is, of course, nothing inevitable about these developments - they are politically determined and can be politically undetermined. In terms of law and order policy, the punitive impulse has in the past quickly met a cost barrier - since imprisonment is not cost-effective, the costs it imposes have always proved inhibiting even for governments committed to an ideology of punishment. Already, Howard's "prison works" decree has produced a very high prison population in this country. It is, of course, possible that Western "liberal" democracy has reached a new era in its response to crime where expense is no barrier. Lilly and Knepper (1992) report that the United States prison population increased from 330,000 in 1980 to 770,000 by 1993. They go on to suggest that the growth of a corrections-commercial complex may be related to the search for alternative markets by firms in the military-industrial complex suffering from the end of the "Cold War". They hypothesise that the "peace dividend" may be used to fund developments in the crime prevention and private corrections markets. This raises the intriguing possibility that a rising prison population may in future be seen not as an unfortunate drain on the public purse but an acceptable way for a non-interventionist government to fuel recovery in a failing capitalist economy! Certainly, at the very least, the development of a commercial interest in punishments would add one more obstacle to a return to a less punitive response to crime.

There has been speculation on whether the moment of "welfarism" has now passed irrevocably as we move into a "post-modern" era. Parton cites Bauman (1992) as identifying the most conspicuous social division as the one between seduction and repression - seduction is the paramount tool of social integration and repression is reserved as the "tool of regulation for the growing numbers on the margins of society who cannot be absorbed into market dependency" (Parton, 1994; 28). The new right and neo-liberal critiques of welfare left social work "particularly vulnerable to criticism and reconstruction as it could be seen to personify all that was problematic in welfarism" (Parton, 1994; 23). Parton (1994) identifies the features of managerialism as characteristic of this reconstruction and concludes that in this analysis the prospects for social work appear bleak.

However, there are also signs of disillusionment with seduction into market dependency and new interest in collective, if more responsive, welfare provision. The period of hegemony enjoyed by the new right and its New Public Management approach may be nearing its end. If a new collectivism were to develop, one of the obstacles to be overcome would be the legacy of managerialism in the civil service and the public services. There is a generation of Civil Servants and service managers who have been taught to believe that NPM is the only approach to public service manage-ment. There are also front-line staff who have only worked under conditions of NPM and who would need to learn to manage their work without prescriptive standards and detailed guidance.

In this book on probation values, part of my brief is to consider the extent to which probation service management reflects "probation values". I have always had some sympathy with critics who challenged the certainty that a discrete set of social work (Timms, 1983; Shardlow, 1989) or probation values (Faulkner, 1989) exists and has been satisfactorily defined. However, if Brian Williams in his introductory chapter has succeeded in setting out a contemporary account of "probation values", then it must be clear that these differ fundamentally from the values underlying current government policy, both generally and as specifically applied to the probation service. Since the New Public Management is an inherent part of the government's tune and requires its managers to dance accordingly, there is little chance that today's probation managers can openly espouse these "probation values". Given a change of tune, it may be possible to resume the search for the right style of management for the probation service.

References

ACOP "More Demanding than Prison" (A Discussion Paper), Wakefield, ACOP, 1988

ACOP/CCPC/NAPO Probation - the next five years, 1987

ACOP/CCPC/NAPO Audit Commission The Probation Service: *Promoting Value for Money*, HMSO, 1989

Audit Commission *Going Straight: Developing Good Practice in the Probation Service*, HMSO, Occasional paper 16 1991

Bauman, Z. *Intimations of Post-modernity*, Routledge, 1992

Beaumont, B. "Privatisation: A Time to be Alert", *Social Work Today*, 23.3.87

Bochel, D. *Probation and Aftercare: Its Development in England and Wales,* Edinburgh, Scottish Academic Press, 1976

Boswell, G. "Supervision in a Changing Organisation", *Probation Journal*, 33, 1986; 135-137

Bowyer, P. "Resource Management Information System (RMIS)", *NAPO News*, April 1992

Brody, S. The Effectiveness of Sentencing: A Review of the Literature, *Home Office Research Study No 35*, HMSO, 1976

Butterworth Report *Report of the Butterworth Inquiry into the Work and Pay of Probation Officers and Social Workers*, Cmnd 5076, HMSO, 1972

Culpitt, I. *Welfare and Citizenship: Beyond the Crisis of the Welfare State*, Sage, 1992

Drakeford, M. "Privatisation, Punishment and the Future for Probation" *Probation Journal*, 35, 1988 , 43-47

Efficiency Unit. *Efficiency Scrutiny of Government Funding for the Voluntary Sector*, HMSO, 1990

Errington, J. "Proceedings from the Second Seminar; Partnership in Dealing with Offenders in the Community Consultations", NCH, 1990

Faulkner, D. "The Future of the Probation Service: A View from Government" in Shaw, R. & Haines, J. (eds) *The Criminal Justice System: A Central Role for the Probation Service*, Cambridge, Institute of Criminology, 1989

Fielder, M. "Purchasing and Providing Services for Offenders: Lessons from America" in Statham, R. & Whitehead, P. (eds) *Managing the Probation Service*, Harlow, Longman, 1991

Gardner, E. "Proceedings from the First Seminar; Partnership in Dealing with Offenders in the Community Consultations", NCH, 1990

Harman, J. "The Quest for Stronger Probation Management: Threat or Opportunity" in Senior, P and Woodhill, D (eds) *Criminal Justice in the 1990's*, Sheffield, PAVIC, 1990

Haxby, D. *Probation: A Changing Service*, Constable, 1978

Home Office, *Probation Service in England and Wales: Statement of National Objectives and Priorities*, Home Office, 1984a

Home Office, The Probation Rules, SI 647, HMSO, 1984b

Home Office, *Efficiency Scrutiny of the Probation Inspectorate*, Home Office, 1987

Home Office, *Punishment, Custody and the Community*, Cmnd 424, London, HMSO, 1988a

Home Office, *Private Sector Involvement in the Remand System*, HMSO, 1988b

Home Office, *The Parole System in England and Wales,* (The Carlisle Report), HMSO, 1988c

Home Office Crime, *Justice and Protecting the Public*, Cmnd. 965, HMSO, 1990a

Home Office, *Supervision and Punishment in the Community; A Framework for Action*, Cmnd. 966, HMSO , 1990b

Home Office, *Partnership in Dealing with Offenders in the Community* Discussion Paper, Home Office, 1990c

Home Office, *Organising Supervision and Punishment in the Community: A Decision Document,* HMSO, 1991a

Home Office, *Partnership in Dealing with Offenders in the Community: A Decision Document*, Home Office, 1991b

Hood, C. "A Public Management for all Seasons", *Public Administration*, 69, 1991; 3-19,

Humphrey, C. "Calling on the Experts: The Financial Management Initiative (FMI), Private Sector Management Consultants and the Probation Service", *Howard Journal*, 30, 1991; 1-18

JNC Report of the Working Party on Management Structure in the Probation and After-care Service, JNC , 1980

Kay, R. "Developing Partnerships between the Probation Service and Voluntary Sector", *NAPO News*, November 1992

Kemshall, H. "Are We All Accountants Now? Financial Management in the Probation Service", *Probation Journal*, 40, 1993a; 2-8

Kemshall, H. "Quality: Friend or Foe?" *Probation Journal*, 40, 1993b; 122-126

King, J. (3rd ed) *The Probation and After-care Service*, Butterworths, 1969

Lewis, P. "Learning from Industry: Macho Management or Collaborative Culture" *Probation Journal*, 38, 1991; 81-85

Lilly, J. R. & Knepper, P. "An International Perspective on the Privatisation of Corrections", *Howard Journal*, 31, 1992; 147-191

Lloyd, C. *Response to SNOP*, Cambridge, Institute of Criminology, 1986

Lovett, C. "Proceedings from the Fourth Seminar; Partnership in Dealing with Offenders in the Community Consultations", NCH, 1991

McWilliams, W. "The rise and development of management thought" in Statham, R. & Whitehead, P. (eds) *Managing the Probation Service*, Harlow, Longman, 1992

Martinson, R. "What Works? Questions and Answers about Prison Reform", *The Public Interest*, 35, 22-54 ,1974

Matthews, R. "New Directions in the Privatisation Debate?", *Probation Journal*, 37, 1990; 50-59

May, T . *Probation: Politics, Policy and Practice*, Buckingham, OUP, 1991

National Audit Office, *Home Office: Control and Management of Probation Services in England and Wales*, HMSO , 1989

NAPO. "Home Office Statement on the Probation Service - NAPO's Response", NAPO, 1984

NAPO. "Punishment, Custody and the Community: The Response of the National Association of Probation Officers", NAPO, 1988

NAPO *et al* . "Framework for Partnership Between Voluntary Organisations and Probation Staff", NAPO, 1990

Nellis, M. "Probation, the State and the Independent Sector" in Senior, P. & Woodhill, D. *Criminal Justice in the 1990's*, Sheffield, PAVIC, 1990

Parry-Khan, L. *Management by Objectives in Probation*, Norwich, UEA Social Work Monographs, 1988

Parton, N. "Problematics of Government, (Post) Modernity and Social Work", *British Journal of Social Work*, 24, 1994, 9-32

Raine, J. & Willson, M. *Managing Criminal Justice*, Hemel Hempstead, Harvester Wheatsheaf, 1993

Rees, H. & Hall Williams, E. (eds) *Punishment, Custody and the Community; Reflections and Comments on the Green Paper*, LSE, 1989

Ryan, M. & Ward, T. "Restructuring, Resistance and Privatisation in the Non-Custodial Sector", *Critical Social Policy*, 30, 1991; 54-67

Sarkis, A. "Power Balances", *NAPO News*, Dec/Jan 1992/1993

Shardlow, S. *The Values of Change in Social Work*, Tavistock/Routledge, 1989

Shaw, R. "Corporate Management in Probation" in Statham, R. & Whitehead, P. (eds) *Managing the Probation Service*, Harlow, Longman (1992)

Shaw, R. & Haines, J. (eds) *The Criminal Justice System: A Central Role for the Probation Service*, Cambridge, Institute of Criminology, 1989

Smith, G. "Professional Reactions and Comments (3)" in Rees, H. & Hall Williams, E. (eds) *Punishment, Custody and the Community*, LSE, 1989

Statham, R. "Towards Managing the Probation Service" in Statham, R. & Whitehead, P. (eds) *Managing the Probation Service*, Harlow, Longman, 1992

Stern, V. "Proceedings from the First Seminar; Partnership in Dealing with Offenders in the Community Consultations", NCH, 1990

Thomas, R. & Vanstone, M. "Leadership in the Middle", *Probation Journal*, 39, 1992; 19-23

Timms, N. *Social Work Values: An Enquiry*, Routledge and Kegan Paul, 1983

Vanstone, M. & Seymour, B. "Probation Service Objectives and the Neglected Ingredients", *Probation Journal*, 33, 1986; 43-48

Walker, H. & Beaumont, B. *Probation Work: Critical Theory and Socialist Practice*, Oxford, Blackwell, 1981

Walker, H. & Beaumont, B. (eds) *Working with Offenders*, Basingstoke, BASW/Macmillan, 1985

Whitehead, P. "Management Information Systems in Probation" in Statham, R. & Whitehead, P. (eds) *Managing the Probation Service*, Harlow, Longman, 1992

Whitehorn, K. "Invent me a word for it"(16.5.93) and "Nappies are the bottom line" (30.5.93), *Observer*, 1993

FOUR: BEYOND BEFRIENDING
OR PAST CARING?: PROBATION VALUES,
TRAINING AND SOCIAL JUSTICE

Jon Arnold and Bill Jordan

As one might expect in a service whose historical roots were in evangelical Christianity, probation officers debate values and the training of new recruits with an almost religious fervour. Conference agendas and the literature of the service are packed with items on these topics. It is as if values might provide a reliable lifejacket (a form of secular salvation) for a service being swept along on the flood of legislative and administrative change.

There are some urgent reasons for these debates. In an article in the Independent on Sunday (5.12.93), it was reported that the Minister of State at the Home Office had mused that the government "have got to do something about the type of people we employ as probation officers". The implication was that the service was out of sympathy with the government's crackdown on crime; a symptom of this disenchantment was the 25 per cent reduction in the numbers sponsored for Diploma in Social Work courses. These speculations have continued, with rumours that the probation service will be recast as "corrections officers", and may be required to wear uniforms. Training is indeed coming under new scrutiny, with an 'independent' review of existing arrangements. The information available at the time of writing this chapter points towards a twin-track system, with a fast lane for 100 recruits per year to do Masters courses at a few "centres of excellence", and the rest to do more applied criminal justice studies.

In one respect, these developments are hardly surprising. All the major social services (and much of the rest of the public sector) have been restructured since the mid-1980's. The roles of both staff and service users have been redefined, they have been given new names, and their responsibilities to each other redrawn. However, the changes to the criminal justice system were among the last, and they have been hastily amended (in 1993) to take account of unintended consequences.

We will argue that these most recent measures, and the hints of further changes for probation, signal deep anxieties about the project of the Thatcher years rather than its further progress. Greater reliance on enforcement and punishment was not part of the New Right's blue print for a dynamic society, but the failure of the deregulated economy to provide adequate rewards, incentives and opportunities for a large group of the population has necessitated these adjustments to the plan, because of the undesirable social consequences of its programme.

The probation service is - not for the first time - debating these issues in terms of a dichotomy between its longstanding social work values and the demands of penal policy. In this chapter, we will try to avoid rehearsing the traditional terms of these debates, and focus instead on some of the reasons for this crisis (occurring in the context of a new "moral panic" about crime). We will argue that the implications for societal values of this crisis go far deeper than the criminal justice system.

ORIGINS

Probation values are closely linked to the service's identity, and to its historical evolution within an institutional and ideological cluster of reforming principles of the twentieth century.

Although these values could be traced to earlier practices (eg., the prison chaplains of the nineteenth century or even eighteenth century) they emerged - originally with the Probation of Offenders Act, 1907 - within the criminal justice system as part of the New Liberal collectivism of the first decade of the century (Vincent and Plant, 1984). The service waxed in the era of post-World War II reforms, and its organisation and methods were based on the assumptions of that period - universal social citizenship, full employment, economic growth. It represented - and considered itself - a progressive wedge in the far older, authoritarian structures of the courts, police and prisons.

To understand the service's current dilemmas, it is necessary to appreciate the very different ideological and organisational origins of the police and prison systems. They developed in the first half of the nineteenth century, and were strongly influenced by the followers of Jeremy Bentham, such as Edwin Chadwick (Leisering, 1990). They reflected the growth of concerns for security and discipline in the increasingly diversified and complex society of rapidly industrialising Britain (Luhmann, 1979). The assumptions they made about social relations were quite different. The infliction of pain (increasingly privation of normal pleasures rather than physical torment) was seen as the most powerful instrument of public policy, and the main means of controlling a residuum amongst the poor, with no stake in the commercial order. Social surveillance, detection and punishment were the characteristic features of reformed institutions for regulating social relations.

New Liberal collectivism did not replace the penology of Benthanism; it took root in the probation service and in some sentencing and penal practices, side by side with that older tradition. These two systems of ideas and organisation have co-existed throughout this century, and both have influenced policy and practice in every part of the criminal justice system. For instance, Sir Alexander Paterson's reforming principles shaped the development of the Borstal system and touched the prison service also (Forsythe, 1991), while ideas of "community policing" have influenced some constabularies in the 1980s, following the Scarman Report.

The two traditions represent different faces of liberalism. They share a perception of society as made up of autonomous individuals engaged in economic and political activity which is both competitive and co-operative. The younger tradition maintains that co-operative social relations can be achieved by giving citizens the material and cultural resources for participation in the public sphere, and by addressing specific problems of co-operation and co-ordination through enlightened expertise (including various kinds of professional practice). The older relies on hierarchies of control, on detailed regulations and prohibitions, disciplinary procedures, surveillance and punishment. Within the criminal justice system, the two have grown together and intertwined so as to be impossible to disentangle.

None the less, they do emerge as antagonistic principles in times of rapid change. Ever since the mid-1960s, governments attempting to impose new duties on the probation service, or to shift the balance between autonomous professional practice and statutory surveillance or regulation, have been resisted by appeals to the service's traditional (i.e. voluntaristic, persuasive, "positive") values. The conflict also comes to the surface in struggles between an increasingly managerialist hierarchy and basic-grade officers. But it should not be forgotten that the service in England and Wales fought hard to stay outside the local authority social services departments in the late 1960s, forming an expedient alliance with the Conservative Party to emphasise its close links with the courts and the judicial process, and that the present emphasis on separate probation identity and training needs (imposed by the Home Office on CCETSW) stemmed partly from consumer surveys amongst probation students and officers (Davies and Wright, 1989).

This chapter argues that the tension between these two elements in the probation service's history has recently grown more acute because of a crisis in the Conservative party's radical programme of social reconstruction. In the early 1980's, the criminal justice system as a whole (and especially the police) were favourably treated in terms of resourcing and political protection, while other social services were first discredited and then restructured along new lines. Now, with the moral panic about law and order and the Back to Basics programme, the spotlight is on criminal justice. We will argue that this reflects a failure of the "property-owning democracy", and a reversion to enforcement-orientated policies (Jordan, forthcoming).

This turmoil has provoked a more sophisticated debate about probation values and training that no longer relies on a crude opposition between social work and punishment, and tries instead to specify the features of good practice, and how these can best be nurtured. However, we will argue that aspects of the older conflict between the rival traditions are inescapable, and should be recognised. The new manageralism is in many ways a thinly-disguised version of Benthamism, and the punishment orientation of the Criminal Justice Act 1991 gives implicit recognition to the fact that the service now focuses on an "underclass" with neither opportunities nor inducements to participate in the economic mainstream. This means that the probation service cannot rely on traditional methods to implement traditional values. It must choose between adopting (and relying exclusively upon) the policies and practices that have become fashionable in the Home Office, or reinterpreting these ideas, and developing innovatory ones of its own.

CRISIS

The Thatcher governments of 1979-90 were in many ways the most radical since 1945, but the prime minister appealed to old values - liberty, independence, responsibility, choice - to justify her programme. Her attack on the welfare state focused on the unintended consequences of collective systems, especially for the disadvantaged, and claimed that they would benefit in the long run from new policies for privatisation, deregulation and restructuring. In this sense, law and order were not central to her programme, except in so far as measures against the trade unions required draconian enforcement (e.g., the miners' strike). It was assumed that, as the reforms dissolved the distortions of social democracy, a whole set of new opportunities and incentives would draw individuals into markets and self-reliant families - the twin pillars of the 'spontaneous order' constituting property-owning democracy.

If this programme had been successful, the criminal justice system might have been one of the few public sector spheres to be sheltered from radical institutional restructuring. It even looked as if practitioners might be allowed to develop "progressive" projects. In the early 1980s, for example, the Criminal Justice Act 1982 limited custodial sentences on young offenders, and the field of youth justice was left to professionals - social workers, educationists and police as well as probation officers - to develop new policies for reducing the use of custody. Even when other forms of social work were being systematically discredited, the government encouraged these initiatives in the field of criminal justice, allowing workers in this field to believe that they were relatively protected from this kind of critical scrutiny. However, rising crime rates and evidence of increased fear of crime meshed with other signs of moral malaise - single parenthood, benefit fraud, truancy, alcoholism and drug abuse, football hooliganism - in the late Thatcher years, and gave rise to a series of moral panics in 1993. What was originally presented as a programme for self-enforcing social relations quickly came to need more overt measures of enforcement, and expenditure on criminal justice rose more rapidly than any other public budget. First the ideal of a shrinking state gave way to a strong central system of direction, then the Criminal Justice Act of 1991 focused on punishment, and recently issues of youth justice in particular have attracted detailed critical comments from ministers. The criminal justice system has become an important site for restructuring and ideological attention, with punishment the focus of the policy agenda.

This cycle of change in the values of the Thatcher programme is like a very speeded-up film of Britain in the nineteenth century, with its shift from optimistic assumptions about the social consequences of economic liberalisation to the punitive pessimism of social Darwinism. It also reflects the fundamental ambivalence of liberalism towards freedom, its supposedly central value. On the one hand there has been the strong endorsement of liberty as the core element in a capsule of political rights necessary for human flourishment, the emphasis in John Stuart Mill, T.H. Green, and their twentieth century followers. But Bentham, Herbert Spencer and others recognised that the 'negative freedoms' of liberalism - prohibitions against interference in the lives and choices of others - still required considerable constraints and regulatory actions.

It is striking that the distinguished contemporary defender of liberalism against its authoritarian adversaries, Stephen Holmes, lists security as the first principle of liberalism, echoing Bentham, not Mill (Holmes, 1993, p.4).

Is security a value? If individual life is sacred, and property is - as liberalism since Locke insists - an entitlement of persons who make themselves, improve their world, and contribute to others' welfare in the process, then presumably the protection of physical beings and their material possessions is indeed at the heart of individual freedom. Yet it was Hobbes, not Locke, who made security his first principle of political society, and justified the Leviathan authority of the state that threatens all its members with its sword. The rule of law, the talisman of 'liberation', justifies spending more on criminal justice than social welfare in California today, and permits outlays of £80,000 for each new British prison cell at a time when public housing programmes are virtually frozen.

Perhaps the central contradiction within the liberal ideology is the notion that people are rationally motivated by material inducements - they think and act instrumentally and strategically as economic agents - yet they are required to treat others with the respect due to beings whose lives and goods are sacred (Durkheim, 1933). Erving Goffman has taught us that the exchange of ritual respect ('face work') is indeed the basis of human communication, and thus of all social relations; we give and save face as much in the marketplace as in the political forum, when we trade with each other as persons (Goffman, 1969). But the cult of the individual also promotes privacy, division and exclusion, and thus an impersonal system of atomised social relations - ideal conditions for opportunistic, exploitative or violently predatory social relations, whether by capitalists towards workers or criminals towards victims. When people have no instrumental reasons for treating each other as fellow citizens, and no material stake in relationships of production and exchange, they develop strategies of predation, defection or extortion, which are facilitated by the pluralistic environment, social divisions and inequalities of the liberal polity.

The main weakness of the Thatcher government's programme of reforms was the lack of material inducements for poor people to participate in the official economy. Deregulation of the labour market, and the destructive power of global forces on British industry, combined to devastate the employment of unskilled workers, and create a new casualised, fragmented economy, where bits and pieces of part-time and short-term employment, combined with undeclared cash work while claiming benefits, became the norm in some districts, while drugs-related crime constituted the economic activity of others.

Government policy treated criminals as economising agents who calculated the costs and benefits of crime and law abiding behaviour (Becker, 1968; Cornish and Clarke, 1986; Stone,1992). Its whole approach, encapsulated in the Criminal Justice Act, 1991, was to set the price of crime high enough to deter all but the reckless and incompetent, but to keep penalties sufficiently 'community-based' to avoid excessive costs to taxpayers. By 1993 it was apparent there had been a miscalculation. Because of the decline in payoffs from legal economic activity (due to the collapse of the official labour market in many deprived districts) criminal activity had become far more attractive at current prices. Hence the switch away from community penalties, and onto far more expensive deterrent custodial sentences.

The moral panics of 1993 represented nemesis overtaking a government that had demonstrated hubris in its claim to be able to restructure society around the two basic institutions of market and family. It was naïve to assume that the new market orientation could substitute for old loyalties and ties; it was dangerous to create conditions of anomie, and hypocritical then to blame parents, schools and social workers for the consequences.

The symbolic watershed for the government was the murder of Jamie Bulger. The symbolism of a small child, taken from his mother in a shopping complex by two boys who were themselves still at primary school, and brutally murdered in a public wasteland, was too poignant. Markets and families did not provide spontaneous social order. Shopping malls were not the civilising element in a commercial society, the substitute for churches and temples.

Two boys dragging a toddler along the bank of a canal did not constitute a family, whose natural sympathies could be relied upon. If no one looked after open spaces and railway lines, and no one took responsibility for the public actions of people in public places, then what happened there was often nasty and brutish, and sometimes protracted.

The moral panic about security in Britain is not a return to basic values, but a recognition that the Thatcher experiment has failed. The new structures and systems are not self-enforcing; they have produced a new set of strategic actions which are in many ways more socially damaging and disturbing than the old. The government must choose between increased enforcement - raising the price of deviance by more incarceration, workfare, training and so on - or a whole new approach to social relations.

ALTERNATIVES

So far this chapter has argued that the new managerialism of the probation service should be understood as implementing policies that have become necessary because of the failure of the Thatcher economic 'miracle'. Because it is in line with the oldest beliefs and values of the criminal justice system, and takes its methods and substance from the Benthamite tradition, it is easy to reconcile with the punishment orientation that re-emerged in 1993. If security becomes the central concern of the British government, then expense is no object: enforcement becomes an end in itself. The other values of the liberal tradition may be allowed to flourish in other fields - even in services for children, where the 1989 legislation is surprisingly positive and enabling in some respects - but not in the sphere of criminal justice. Managerialism thus shifts its focus from efficiency (value for money) and technocratic service delivery (packages of penalties) towards power and punishment. Practice must be the detailed implementation of central government policy for the surveillance and control of the dangerous classes.

Of course it is not as simple as this. In a pluralistic society, public agencies contain a diversity of interest groups, competing for power, forming new alliances, splitting from old allies, developing new discourses (Parton, 1994). Managerialism is not central government made flesh, any more than practice can ever be nothing but policy made flesh. Each probation service will interpret the framework of laws, regulations and objectives differently, and each team will implement this interpretation in its own style, embodying resistance to power as well as compliance with it. This gives opportunities for putting a positive spin on even the most repressive regime, and for developing innovatory practices that turn the intentions of legislators and managers on their heads. Just as offenders can subvert programmes for training or treatment, so practitioners can use the rhetoric of punishment to justify and elaborate projects with quite a different emphasis.

So it is important to analyse the directions that alternative practices can take, and the values that should inform new interpretations. A good deal of work has already been done by the intellectual community that constitutes probation studies, and by practitioners in the field, to clarify these issues. Our purpose in this chapter is to identify some of the pitfalls in these developments, and suggest alternatives.

One strong feature of the new literature is the critique of "traditional probation values" as a basis for resistance to managerialism, and of genericism (in training and in ideology) as a foundation for alternative practices. According to this view - of which Mike Nellis (1993a, 1993b) is a persuasive advocate - vague, general principles like "respect for persons" have little to offer because they do not counter managerialist imperatives, and because they allow a focus on individual problems at the expense of structural and power-orientated analyses. The task is thus seen as the production of a far more specific set of values and principles that are of direct relevance to the criminal justice field, and that address the changes in political authority, economic structure and social relations that have occurred in Britain. This means moving away from ethical codes and professional guidance, focusing instead on the harder-edged criminological developments of recent years, and the practice innovations that have proved themselves in the field.

Nellis's provisional list of values is (a) anti-custodialism - the minimisation of unnecessary imprisonment, and the insistence on the harmful effects of custody; (b) restorative justice - mediation and other forms of negotiated, informal conflict resolution, within a rehabilitative and socially integrative framework; and (c) community safety - the reduction of vulnerability and anxiety among "at risk" populations. This is certainly a different list from the present-day social-work-value base, with its contradictory juxtaposition of Kantian (individualistic) principles, professional ethics and anti-oppressive (power-analytic) maxims. It focuses on the criminal justice system itself, and the particular victimology of British crime, and seeks to distil values from best practice in a number of related fields.

To us, this list seems too specific, and to miss links with traditional "probation values" that can be easily made. Furthermore, it runs the risk of isolating probation from a far more extensive range of professional, informal and every-day practices in wider society. Indeed, it could move too far towards managerialism in its overtones of justice-orientated technocracy. We would argue that probation cannot afford to become cut-off from an overall project of social justice, voluntary co-operation, the reciprocity of free and equal fellow-citizens, democratic participation and public service for the common good. Its origins were in just such a project, it had some historical success in humanising the criminal justice system as part of that social movement, and now above all times it needs to keep its links with that tradition.

It is useful to specify values relating to particular areas of practice, but not in an exclusive way: these should be a "second tier", below more general values from the broader field of political and moral thought. It is also important to recognise potential conflicts between the principles on Nellis's list. Anti-custodialism is in some jeopardy at present as a practice, not only because of the government's emphasis on punishment, but also because of its neglect of the communities from which offenders come. By focusing too exclusively on system issues and policies - diversion, avoidance of net-widening and deviance-amplification, etc - it is in danger of isolating itself in a technocratic criminal justice backwater, as unpopular with desperate parents and irate neighbours as with punitive rhetoricians. It is not obvious how anti-custodialism links with restorative justice: these links have to be actively constructed. "Community safety" is really a very polite and collectivist term for liberal security. If restorative justice cannot find positive ways of building communities and righting wrongs, then safety and security will always fall back on punishment, and the collective consequences of anti-custodialist decisions will come back to haunt systems-orientated professionals.

TRAINING

These issues have been faithfully reflected in the tensions between the Home Office and the Central Council for Education and Training in Social Work (CCETSW). Up to now, the outcome has been a compromise: in the Diploma in Social Work (DipSW) formula for the 1990s, the probation service has been allowed to become much more actively involved in training, and to follow what has mainly been an instrumentalist agenda for specific role preparation, while CCETSW has simultaneously imposed a more explicit - if confused and confusing (Jordan *et al*, 1993) - agenda for social work values and ethics.

This compromise mirrors the struggles over training in the 1980s, culminating in the University of East Anglia's consumer surveys of probation students and newly appointed officers (Davies and Wright, 1989) and the Coleman Review of training courses. The Home Office initiated both of these exercises with a mind that was far from open; indeed, criticisms of the consumer survey focused on the fact that it found - by dubious methodology - what its sponsors were well known to believe, that courses provided too much education in critical analysis of social relations and social policy, and too little training in law, penology and probation practice (Hardiker and Willis, 1989). It was also an open secret that the Home Office and local probation managers had become uneasy about personalist teaching methods (experiential learning) and the social justice orientation of college staff, and wanted to see the more technical aspects of the work taught, if necessary in didactic ways, and with more of a criminal justice orientation.

At the root of these tensions was the more fundamental cleavage between two approaches to training and to probation work itself. On the one side stood a value commitment to respect for persons and optimism about the possibilities of personal growth and change; on the other, technical methods of containment or control or punishment, combined with scepticism about change. Training based on the former values has, with some justification, been accused of woolliness and lack of precision, for instance over evaluation of effectiveness. Training based on the latter is certainly more measurable (like the practice it promotes), but tends to be rigid and mechanical (Hardiker and Willis, 1989), and may lead to practice that is counter-productive. Drakeford's (1993) analysis of breach proceedings argues that the inflexible and punitive interpretation of standards of compliance that has characterised recent practice in probation and community service actually discredits community-based penalties and contributes to a "culture of pessimism" about the possibilities of rehabilitation (Carson, 1990; Lloyd, 1992).

On the face of it, the compromise embodied in the DipSW offers the possibility of the best of both worlds. A tougher-minded personalist agenda might insist that growth-orientated training methods are more rigorously assessed, just as counselling methods of practice should be. At the same time, critical evaluation of the technocratic developments in probation policy and practice could use the skills of social scientific analysis, and the imaginative capacities developed through study. Above all, training staff - both college-based and practice teacher - could model the theory practice integration that is the enduring holy grail of training, and develop the autonomous competence of students through participatory adult learning.

Unfortunately, there is some evidence (as yet mainly anecdotal) of the opposite tendency, towards the worst of all worlds, and that this is focused on probation more than other social work training. Although this is only one site of these problems, we shall use the example of anti-discriminatory and anti-oppressive practice to show what we mean by this, because it is such an important element in CCETSW's values requirements for the DipSW programme.

CCETSW's Paper 30 makes it clear that sensitive but firm anti-discriminatory work is an essential social work competence, and probation services now have written policies on many of the issues.

Students are required to demonstrate an awareness of, and ability to challenge, discrimination and oppression. These are demanding standards: they must learn to recognise how power and prejudice combine to produce exclusion, subordination and stigma, both at the individual and institutional levels.

Mutual respect and trust (both between staff and students, and within the student group) seem essential features of the learning environment in which such issues are tackled. As with other competences that require personal growth and change, challenging racism or sexism is most successfully achieved within a culture of openness to learning, and a shared spirit of supportiveness and commitment. The aim should be that all can learn from each other, where all share an interest in raising standards of practice. Sharp disagreements and painful insights are far more effective educational tools where challenges and criticisms can be perceived as aimed at improving everyone's practice, rather than scoring points off each other.

Such a culture and environment have to be created. While personalist approaches can be misused for oppressive purposes, instrumentalist, didactic methods that discount sharing and trust are clearly inadequate. Worse still, a service that relies on hierarchical power and coercion in its every-day relationships between manage-ment and staff, and with its clients, provides the least promising model of such an environment. Within such a culture, challenges are most likely to take the form of angry accusations, to deal in political correctness rather than personal learning, and to contribute to unresolvable tensions or long-running disputes between members.

Anti-discriminatory and anti-oppressive practice are currently the radical cutting edge of the social work training agenda, and the most controversial element in CCETSW's requirements. But, instead of being a stimulating site for theory: practice integration, there is a danger that this will become a sterile battleground for formalistic points-scoring, with the radical message - about power, equality and inclusion - totally lost. This is a special danger in the probation setting, where a thorough going interpretation of the anti-oppressive agenda would challenge almost every element of the Home Office's policies, procedures and practices, but where a narrow focus on the instrumentalities of specific issues merely reinforces the oppressive aspects of the culture.

However, all the above considerations apply to the rest of the training curriculum also, albeit less dramatically. In the DipSW's model of 'partnership' between colleges and agencies, students are the excluded third party. Disputes over the relative importance of critical and reflective educational processes and skills-orientated apprenticeship have produced a credentialist checklist compromise, that can lead to an emphasis on assessment at the expense of learning, and a replication in the classroom of many of the more questionable features of the service itself. Above all, students can experience themselves as being managed and processed, criticised and evaluated, as being given technical instruction, but not as being participants in a creative, developing and supportive culture, to which they can make a positive contribution.

CONCLUSIONS

Disputes about values are notoriously difficult to settle, and many may regard them as part of an ideological superstructure that has little relevance to the 'realities' of everyday practice. However, there is increasing evidence - sufficient to convince hard-nosed social scientists, including economists - that the culture in which individuals interact is the most important determinant of the outcomes of their interaction. Furthermore, researchers now claim that this is as true of economic outcomes - rates of growth of production and income - and of crime rates, as it is of political efficiency and quality of life (Putnam, 1993, ch.6).

The argument can be framed in exactly the terms favoured by the British government and the Home Office - microeconomic analysis, rational choice and public choice theory. The problem of order is also a problem of trust (Gambetta, 1988). Why should I co-operate with you (or anyone else) if I know that your best strategy is to exploit my willingness to meet you halfway, and play me for a sucker? This "Prisoner's Dilemma" formulation underpinned Thomas Hobbes's famous account of the state of nature, and his insistence that the only viable form of 'social contract' between individuals who had no reason to trust each other was to appoint a third party (the sovereign state) to provide justice, under threat of punishment.

The trouble with Hobbes's solution (his version of 'back to basics' after the turmoil of the English Civil War) is that his third party is neither neutral nor cost free. Powerful interest groups can capture the state, and frame its rules to their advantage. There is little to restrain such actors from driving up and up the price of enforcement, requiring some citizens to pay higher taxes, and others longer terms of imprisonment. One need look no further than the United States for examples.

A far more economic solution is for citizens to trust each other and co-operate in self-enforcing ways. Research shows that this occurs where there are numerous dense networks of voluntary associations (including sports, leisure and cultural clubs) and a culture of 'civic engagement' (Ostrom, 1990; Hirschman, 1984; Coleman, 1990). Consensus about essentials is not a necessary condition for this culture, but some forms of mutual respect, including commitment to discussion, equal political rights and widespread reciprocity are. The trust fostered by habits of co- operation in groups and associations produces a form of social capital, which is expanded, not depleted, by frequent use. This cannot be created from outside (e.g. by the state), but it can be undermined by outside forces.

Reciprocity and trust thrive in communities of autonomous individuals, practising co-operation in "horizontally" structured organisations with shared power. Where trust is lacking, "vertically" structured organisations rely on hierarchy and sanction for order. Individuals cannot trust each other, so they have to be coerced into keeping agreements. The trouble is that this system of social relations is self-perpetuating: the "clients" of a powerful authority have no reason to trust each other, but instead compete for their patron's favour, while he in turn has every incentive to divide and rule. Putnam shows that there has been an 800 year continuity of such relations in Southern Italy, stemming from the Norman Kingdom of Naples. It has bred a cycle of violent crime, and demands for draconian punishment. No actor has an interest in breaking the cycle; the whole system runs on exploitation, extortion and fear.

By contrast, a democratic community runs on trust, which enables prosperity and flexible growth as well as good government - features which Putnam could show conclusively to stem from the civic culture of regions that had been backward at the turn of the century (Putnam, 1993, ch.5). The implications are clear: we should put a higher value on the social capital produced by all forms of co-operation and association, and evaluate power-based authority - however skilled and knowledgeable - more critically.

Civic trust versus authoritarian enforcement is thus a crucial issue for societies. The choice between the ethics of co-operation, collectivism and social justice on the one hand, and security, surveillance and punishment on the other, is not simply a technocratic issue about "what works" in the field of criminal justice. It can best be addressed in the context of the central values and institutional systems of a democratic society. When probation officers practice, and probation students learn, they create and use cultural resources to do so, and the actions are relevant to the quality of social relations in our society.

In the past 15 years, government policy has not merely made the poor and disadvantaged worse off: it has isolated them from other sections of society, and created conflicts of interest between them and the mainstream. The probation service can either seek to sustain the social capital still possessed by the "underclass" - informal systems of co-operation, networks of reciprocity and trust, and a decent culture of respect from public sector workers - or it can contribute to the replacement of civic engagement by power-orientated techniques of control and punishment.

Given the rise in the crime rate, it is questionable whether the probation service is really working with "much more serious" offenders than it was in the generation when we (the authors) were practitioners. It seems far more likely that the sons and daughters of our clients are offending five times as frequently as their parents because they face far more adverse economic and social conditions, with far less support from public services.

Research demonstrated some time ago that probation officers use tougher sanctions against people in more unstable, vulnerable and stressful situations (Lawson, 1978). The challenge for the service in the 1990s is to find ways of offering effective support to such people, to convince them of its goodwill and genuine commitment to their needs, and its concern to promote trust and co-operation in their communities.

References

Becker, G. S., "Crime and Punishment: An Economic Approach", *Journal of Political Economy*, 76, 2, 1968; 169-217

Carson, D. "Reports to Court: A Role in Preventing Decision Error", *Journal of Social Welfare Law*, 3, 1990l 151-63

Coleman, J. S. Foundations of Social Theory, Cambridge, Mass.: Harvard University Press, 1990

Cornish, D. B. & Clarke, R. V. *The Reasoning Criminal: Rational Choice Perspectives on Offending*, New York, Springer-Verlag, 1986

Davies, M. & Wright, A. *Probation Training: A Consumer Perspective*, Norwich: University of East Anglia, 1989

Drakeford, M. "The Probation Service, Breach and the Criminal Justice Act, 1991", *Howard Journal*, 32, 4, 1993; 291-303

Durkheim, E. *The Division of Labour in Society*, New York: Free Press, 1933

Forsythe, W. J. *Reform and Rehabilitation in the English Prison System*, Exeter University Press, 1991

Gambetta, D. (Ed.), *Trust: Making and Breaking Co-operative Relations*, Oxford: Blackwell, 1988

Goffman, E. *Interaction Ritual*, New York:DoubledayAnchor, 1969

Hardiker, P. & Willis, A. "Cloning Probation Officers: Consumer Research and Implications for Training', *Howard Journal*, 28, 4, 1989; 323-9

Hirschman, A.O. *Getting Ahead Collectively: Grass-Roots Experiences in Latin America*, New York: Pergamon, 1984

Holmes, S. *The Anatomy of Anti-Liberalism*, Cambridge, Mass.: Harvard University Press, 1993

Jordan, B. (forthcoming), "Are New Right Policies Sustainable? 'Back to Basics' and Public Choice", *Journal of Social Policy*.

Jordan, B., Karban, K., Mansoor K., Masson, H. & O'Byrne, P. "Teaching Values: An Experience of the Diploma in Social Work", *Social Work Education*, 12, 1, 1993; 7-18.

Lawson, C. *The Probation Officer as Prosecutor: A Study in Proceedings for Breach of Requirements for Probation*, Institute of Criminology, Cambridge University, 1978

Leisering, L. "Social Differentiation and the Formation of Statutory Welfare in England, 1795-1847", Doctoral Thesis, London School of Economics, 1990

Lloyd, C, "National Standards for Community Service Orders: The First Two Years of Operation", *Home Office Research Bulletin*, 31, 1992; 16-21

Luhmann, N. "Differentiation of Society", *Canadian Journal of Sociology*, 2, 1977; 29-53

Nellis, M. "Criminology, Crime Prevention and the Future of Probation Training", in Bottomley, K., Fowles, T. & Rever, R. (Eds.), *Criminal Justice: Theory and Practice, Selected Papers from British Criminology Conference*, 1993a

Nellis, M. "Criminology, Corporatism and Probation Values", Birmingham: University of Birmingham, 1993b

Ostrom, E. *Governing the Commons: The Evolution of Institutions for Collective Action*, Cambridge: Cambridge University Press, 1990

Parton, N. "'Problematics of Government', (Post) Modernity and Social Work", *British Journal of Social Work*, 24, 1994; 9-32

Putnam, R. D. *Making Democracy Work: Civic Traditions in Modern Italy*, Princeton: Princeton University Press, 1993

Stone, N. "Probation in the 1990s: No Escaping Nemesis?" in Williams, B. & Senior, P. (Eds.), *Probation Practice after the Criminal Justice Act, 1991*, Sheffield: PAVIC/Sheffield Hallam University, 1992; 3-20

Vincent, A. & Plant, R. *Philosophy, Politics and Citizenship: The Life and Thought of the British Idealists*, Oxford: Blackwell , 1984

FIVE: PSRs AND NATIONAL STANDARDS: WHO CALLS THE TUNE?

Anne Celnick and Bill McWilliams

The implementation of national standards for pre-sentence reports in 1992 is not the first attempt by the government to promulgate consistent practice to a minimum standard in the preparation of reports for court but it is certainly the most determined. In 1961, the Streatfield Committee (Home Office and Lord Chancellor's Office 1961) set out recommendations concerning both the function of, and the information to be included in, probation reports to the courts. In 1983 (Home Office 1983) and 1986 (Home Office 1986), the Home Office produced circulars giving guidance for probation officers about the appropriate content and style of reports. The difference between these earlier documents and national standards, however, was that the former had the status of guidance and some probation officers may even have been unaware of their existence. In contrast, national standards were required to be implemented, and provision was made to train all relevant staff in their use. National standards, therefore, were presented as mandatory.

The attempt to remove the discretion of probation officers to choose whether or not to follow guidance on report writing was regarded by some as an attack on their values. It could be argued that this is a case of personal and professional values becoming confused. As Harris (1989) points out:

> *"For many years he who paid the piper chose not to call the tune, and in consequence there came into being among many of the pipers the collective delusion that they could actually choose their own tune. Now the tune is being called, really for the first time, and the pipers, though free to play it or not, will make their decision in the knowledge that there are other pipers waiting in the wings and rather keen to take centre stage"* (p55).

Whilst clearly national standards can be seen as an attack on personal values about autonomy, only to the extent that national standards threaten professional values about what is ethically correct or necessary for competent practice can their imposition be regarded as an attack on professional values. That is not to deny the possibility, however, that the intention might be to restrict probation officers' control over the definition of what constitutes 'good' professional practice, independent of governmental views.

VALUES IN REPORT WRITING

As Timms (1983) comments:

"Those elements discussed under the single rubric 'values' are crucial to the conception and practice of social work. However, it is difficult to see how crucial they are, the kind of importance they have, because we try to work with 'values' as a completely undifferentiated notion . . . Almost any kind of belief and obligation, anything preferred for any reason or for no apparent reason at all, any ideal or rule, is heaped into a large pantechnicon carrying the device 'Social Work Values - will travel anywhere'"(2).

He goes on to argue that "value talk is underdeveloped and conversations about values or social work values has hardly started" (p32). This is not the place to embark on a lengthy contribution to such a debate but it is necessary to establish how we shall be using "value" before considering how probation officers' values are affected by national standards.

"Value" and "values" are used in a range of contexts throughout which ideas about what is "good" are interwoven. "Value" may be used a way of describing an object or action (a valuable painting) but "value" or "values" can also be used in the sense of belief or a principle which is used to decide what goals it is "good" to pursue and which are the "good" ways to achieve those goals; and we shall be using "values" in this sense. A value of this kind, like the value of an object or action, can be rooted in economic, technical, utilitarian, aesthetic or moral considerations. We shall distinguish between personal values, which differ from person to person, and professional values, which are those values individuals are expected to espouse when they become members of that profession. However, if they have a choice, it is predictable that people will be unlikely to stay long in a profession whose values they do not share. Equally, if personal and professional values coincide, there may be difficulty in distinguishing which of them are personal and which are professional.

Most of the values commonly referred to as traditional probation values are also social work values and they are mainly moral ones. For example, Weston (1978) speaks of the "unshakeable desire for and faith in the capacity of people to grow and improve in their personal and social functioning" (20). Echoing that view, Bottoms and Stelman (1988) suggest that the three core values of probation are respect for persons, care for persons and hope for the future and recognition of clients' potential for survival and growth. Similarly, Timms suggests that "social work values" should be "reinterpreted as notions of what constitutes human fulfilment, what aids or hinders it, what duties it entails, what ideals it encapsulates and what valuations may be indicated in particular situations" (3). In an empirical study of social inquiry report writing, one of us (McWilliams, 1986) suggested professional beliefs can be classified conveniently into three groups namely: (i) beliefs about impartiality and objectivity; (ii) beliefs about professional expertise in practice; and (iii) beliefs about fairness and justice (405-6).

However, "technical" or utilitarian values relating to competent practice are less often clearly articulated than beliefs about what is ethically good practice.

The reason for the centrality of moral values in probation practice expressed in statements like "[the probation service's] value lies in being a repository for rehabilitative ideals within the criminal justice system" (Cochrane *et al.*, 1993) may be found in David Garland's (1991) proposition that penal institutions, of which the probation service is one example, both represent and play a part in creating society's moral values in relation to the treatment of offenders:

The representations projected by penal practice are not just threats aimed at criminals: they are also positive symbols which help produce subjectivities, forms of authority, and social relations (276).

Thus we find in an article on the values of the probation service greater emphasis being laid on the moral role of the probation officer as "a prime example of the agent of reconciliation between courts and offenders, law-abiding communities and their deviant members" (Boswell and Worthington, 1988, 128) than on beliefs about what exemplifies competent practice.

However, another reason for the emphasis on moral values may be not only that the "core values of the Service are no longer self-explanatory and taken for granted by all" [emphasis added] (Kemshall, 1993, 126) but that dealing humanely with offenders has never been a universally held moral value; on the contrary, many people regard offenders as having excluded themselves from the right to be treated with respect and care. Even at governmental level, there may be, at best, some ambivalence about the role of the probation service as "the humane arm of the criminal justice system" (Boswell and Worthington, 1988, 129); in an interview with "Probation Journal" (Probation Journal 1988), John Patten, a Home Office minister at the time, argued trenchantly but, in our view, unconvincingly (see Celnick, 1989, 302-9) that there was no conflict between punishing and offering help:

" Some people in the Probation Service seem to have a hang-up about language and do not like to be involved in things like punishment . . . I think one wants to forget all inhibitions about language and explain to the general public that one is both punishing, supervising punishment and also supervising and trying to rehabilitate"(81-2).

Consequently, in an environment generally hostile to those seen as criminals, the emphasis on moral values in probation may be the result of a perception that it is necessary to reiterate and reinforce the importance of such values when working with offenders.

To sum up this part of our argument, we take values to be beliefs about what is "good" and we have seen that "good" may be defined in ways other than "ethically good". Beliefs about good, in the sense of competent, probation practice appear to be less frequently articulated than moral values. The traditional moral values are commonly expressed as humane treatment of offenders, care and respect for them and belief in their potential for growth, justice and fairness. Given the equivocal societal attitude to the rights of offenders, these are the values which are most at risk from changes in government policy. In the next section we shall examine whether there is any evidence of an attack on these moral values from national standards for pre-sentence reports.

NATIONAL STANDARDS AND VALUES

The similarities between the 1986 circular giving guidance on the content of social inquiry reports and national standards for pre-sentence reports are considerable, and the two documents differ often only in that national standards spell out the requirements in greater detail. For example, both emphasise the need for the report to be impartial and balanced containing details of both mitigating and aggravating factors, to be clear and concise with no irrelevant details or jargon and with a statement of the sources of information and whether it has been verified or not. None of that would appear to be contentious in theory for probation officers and the official NAPO view (Schofield, 1992) was that national standards on pre-sentence reports "do much to consolidate good report writing practice" (3). Moreover, as reported by one of us in an empirical study (McWilliams, 1986), the objectivity and impartiality required by the standards are confirmed by probation officers to be important, officers commenting that:

"somebody goes out to do as objective a picture as they can to begin with";

"I'm just here to present the facts to court";
"reports should be communication of factual ideas" (422).

The requirement for managers to set up systems for ensuring the quality of reports would also appear to be consistent with values about doing a good job.

National standards for pre-sentence reports not only set out in greater detail how to write a competent report, but they also differ from the 1986 circular in dealing with aspects of report preparation which relate to moral values. For example, there is a new emphasis on anti-discriminatory practice and on the rights of the defendant. The circular merely notes that:

"In cases involving members of ethnic minorities it is especially important for the SIR to bring out any significant aspects of the defendant's social or cultural background which may not otherwise be understood by the court" (para 11).

In contrast, national standards state that PSRs and proposals "must be free of discrimination on the grounds of race, gender, age, disability, language, ability, literacy, religion, sexual orientation or any other improper grounds" (para 4) and also lay a duty on local managements to implement and monitor an equal opportunity policy. Another example which is of relevance to the value of respect for individuals is the national standards requirement that the offender must be given information by the report writer before interview "about possible disclosure of the report" (para 16). Thus far, then, there would appear to be little if any conflict with probation officers' professional values. However, there is one requirement in particular which has provoked controversy and this is to consider the appropriate level of restriction of liberty represented by a community sentence.

Although the expectation that report writers will reach a provisional assessment of seriousness of the offence has also been criticised, this has been largely on the ground of impracticability. For example, Bottoms and Stelman, (1988, 27) agree with Streatfeild that probation officers do not have the training or experience to judge seriousness and Cochrane *et al* (1993) suggest that not only do officers not have the training for the task but judging seriousness would impede other objectives being pursued in the preparation of the report:

"One of the most worrying innovations being drawn from the Act is that the Probation Service, through the pre-sentence

*report, should contribute to the judgements made at this point.
We believe that this is problematic for a number of fundamental
reasons:*

*1. Trust: The information is obtained in a context where the
author is attempting to develop a constructive atmosphere of
trust which will enable possibilities for rehabilitation to be
realistically assessed. If probation reports are likely to be used
negatively in the determination of seriousness then the client
should have the right to legal representation in the interview...*

*2. Professional Judgement: ... [probation officers] are not
trained to make moral judgements about culpability - quite the
reverse. Their very value lies in their training to reframe such
judgements into professional terms"* (10).

More recently, the Association of Chief Officers of Probation, the
Justices' Clerks Society and the Magistrates' Association have
urged courts to give a preliminary indication of seriousness to guide
report writers in their task of proposing a disposition compatible in
terms of restriction of liberty with the court's view. However, that
move is unlikely to make the requirement more acceptable to the
authors of a letter to NAPO News (no. 49, April) in 1992:

*"When we used to put forward recommendations for probation
. . . we always knew that such intervention constituted a
real degree of intrusion into people's lives ... Let us leave the
sentencers to grapple with the issue of "restriction on liberty"
whilst we concentrate on suitability ... [there is] a need for us
to have the courage not to use some of the new language and to
reassert the traditional values of the use of probation. When
we read these new PSRs, somehow the comments on the
restriction on liberty fit uneasily and lack sincerity. Well of
course they do!"* (2).

The "traditional values of [sic] the use of probation" are that
probation was, until the 1991 Criminal Justice Act, not intended as a
punishment but as a suspension of punishment. The purpose of the
order was to advise, assist and befriend the offender in the hope that
it would enable him or her to live within the law. The 1991 Criminal
Justice Act made the probation order just one of a range of
community sentences supervised by the probation service given as
"punishment in the community".

One of us (Celnick, 1989) has explored some of the implications
of this development elsewhere and there is not space to repeat the

argument here. Briefly, however, whilst many might argue that justice required offenders to be punished, many probation officers believe, like Duff (1986), that punishment cannot be given fairly in an unjust society. This is not because punishment is necessarily inconsistent with belief in potential for growth and respect for persons (indeed Duff argues that it promotes those values because it treats the offender as a moral agent) but because, as Duff asserts, punishment can only be justified if the offender has offended against the requirements of a system of law which can properly serve the common good of the community to which she belongs (292).

As Hudson (1987) points out:

"If rewards are unevenly distributed then obligations are also unevenly due and retributive punishment based on desert has no meaning" (169).

For that reason, punishment is in conflict with probation officers' beliefs in justice and fairness. If punishing an offender is regarded as unjust, and to the extent that national standards contain an assumption that the purpose of a pre-sentence report is to assist the judge determine the most suitable punishment, then there is a conflict for probation officers also with the moral values of treating offenders with care and respect.

There remains the question of how national standards impact on professional values related to competence. We have already noted that these are less commonly articulated than moral values but, particularly in relation to report-writing practice, ideas about what makes for a "good" report depend as much on technical competence in such areas as assessment, clarity of expression, presentation of a reasoned case and objectivity as on moral values. In the next section, we shall examine how national standards may affect practice in respect of values about competent practice.

NATIONAL STANDARDS IN PRACTICE

Sentencers (Home Office Inspectorate of Probation 1993) have suggested that the standard of reports presented to them has improved since the implementation of the 1991 Criminal Justice Act; and that may indicate that national standards have facilitated the expression of professional values concerned with competent practice. One of us attempted to check whether this was indeed the case by undertaking a small empirical study comparing pre-sentence reports with social inquiry reports collected for an earlier research project. This research involved the collection of reports prepared for a single Crown Court on defendants aged between 17 and 20 in which the recommendation was for probation, with or without conditions. Thirty pre-sentence reports were collected which matched reports from the social inquiry report sample as closely as practicable in order to exclude differences resulting from the different circumstances of the case.

Reports were matched for gender, court, recommendation/proposal and for age in most cases with no greater difference than one year in the remaining few. Main offences were matched, as closely as possible for type and gravity (using the local guidance on assessing gravity) although associated offences could not always be matched. Although it was not possible to compare PSRs written by the same author as the SIR, some officers (whose experience ranged from over ten years in the service to students on placement) appeared in the sample as both PSR author and SIR author. The resulting sample consisted of fifty-four men and six women between the ages of eighteen and twenty. Twenty reports concerned offences of burglary and the others were fairly evenly spread over the range of offences. All but one were assessed as being in the community sentence or custody threshold band with the majority (forty-two) in the latter category.

It is worth commenting on the possibility of bias created by the method of assessment; reports were compared against a list of features derived from National Standards and an assessment was made of the extent to which a particular report met each standard.

Because it was not possible to disguise which reports were PSRs and which were SIRs, the assessor's preconceptions about the likely result could have biased the judgment. In the event, the assessor was proved wrong in her expectation (on the basis of a belief that national standards were little more than a codification of good practice), that no difference would be found.

Caution has to be exercised in interpreting the results of the comparison between PSRs and SIRs because of the relatively small numbers of reports involved. Nevertheless, where differences between the groups are reported to be statistically significant, there is a reasonable chance that the same differences would have been found in a larger sample.

Detailed description of the methods used in the study and its results can be found elsewhere (Celnick, 1994) and only a broad account of the findings will be reiterated here. In general, there appeared to be some important differences between social inquiry reports and pre-sentence reports which reflected the new requirements of national standards. For example, compared with the social inquiry reports, pre-sentence reports were:

more likely to have been based on seeing prosecution documentation and therefore to contain more verified information;

significantly more likely to discuss seriousness of offence;

significantly more likely to discuss the attitude of offender to the offence;

less likely to contain information unconnected with offending behaviour.

These factors are important in contributing towards effective presentation of a case for a particular proposal, clarity and an appearance of impartiality and, to that extent, may support the view that national standards reinforce professional values rather than conflicting with them. However, that is not to say that social inquiry reports were necessarily less competent in these respects. We reproduce below examples of a social inquiry and pre-sentence report respectively to illustrate that point.

Example of SIR
Introduction
1. *In the preparation of this report I have interviewed K on three occasions in the probation office. I have consulted with colleagues at [probation centre] and have made reference to his previous convictions. I have not heard the evidence for the prosecution. I have supervised his co-accused L for twelve months in the past on a probation order.*

Offending Behaviour
2. *K is charged with an offence of house burglary and two separate thefts from cars. He is pleading not guilty to a further offence of deception which goes to trial today. This report only addresses those offences to which K submits a guilty plea. The burglary of the dwelling house was committed with L against one of L's "friends". K tells me that he had met L a few weeks prior to the offence. K had been working away, renting his accommodation out in his absence. His tenants had not paid the electricity bill and as a consequence his supply had been disconnected. He returned [home] in January when his employment came to an end and found his flat unbearably cold without heating. He could not afford reconnection charges however. L suggested that they burgle an acquaintance's house, as they possessed easily disposable items. (From my contact with L in the past, I would*

verify that this behaviour would not be uncharacteristic.)
The items stolen were sold but I am told did not raise
sufficient funds to cover reconnection of the electricity supply
and was spent on alcohol and socialising instead.

The thefts from cars in March 1990 also occurred with an
experienced offender . . . K tells me that he had been drinking
with his co-accused who broke into two vehicles on the way
home, stealing stereo systems. K's account, [sic] [co-
accused] committed the offences without consulting him. He
took no share in the proceeds of the crime but was arrested
with . . . and subsequently charged.

Social situation in relation to offending
3. *K presents as a young man who has struggled with the*
transition into independent living. He left home at 16 to join
the army after coping with increasingly difficult family rela-
tionships resulting in his parents' divorce. He was discharged
from the army after nine months because of a knee injury. He
describes feeling bitterly disappointed and deeply regretted
having to return home to live with his step-father. He quickly
obtained a Youth Training Scheme place and moved away
from home again in January 1990. His accommodation was
insecure from the outset and eventually he moved into the . . .
Hostel for the homeless and rootless. Obviously this is not the
best environment for an unconfident and somewhat naïve
young man who quickly came under the influence of older
men, some with drink problems, others who had a history of
offending. With little else positive in his life (no employment
or stable relationships) he was at high risk of offending. To his
credit he did find independent accommodation for some time
following the first offences, but did not have the skills
necessary to manage independent living and made the mistake
of sub-letting to irresponsible tenants. He has now returned
to [hostel] where he is due to move into the rehabilitation area
in the next few weeks, where he will learn the independent
living skills he lacked previously. He now acknowledges that
he needs to learn and is keen to do so.

K is currently uneployed. His last job as a worker on the
fairground in . . . expired at the end of the season. He would
like to find full-time work and would welcome any help to do
so.

Conclusion

4. This is K's second Court appearance. Until relatively recently he has been a man of good character. His offending bears a strong correlation with his unsuccessful transition into independent living. He presents as a man with a veneer of self-confidence, but has admitted that he requires help to move his life on in a more constructive direction. If placed on probation today, I envisage covering the following areas:-

1) Employment and training opportunities, motivation and direction into work;

2) In co-operation with [hostel] staff, assisting in equipping K with independent living skills;

3) In co-operation with [education project] arranging adult literacy classes which K admits that he needs;

4) Offending behaviour work - helping K look at his drift into offending, the effect it has on victims and equipping him with social skills to enable him to resist offending in the future. K has agreed to attend the house burglary group to address this problem.

I would recommend this course of action to the Court and believe that the work could be achieved in a twelve-month period. K understands the implications of such a sentence and is highly motivated to comply.

EXAMPLE OF PSR

Sources of report

In order to prepare this report I have interviewed J on one occasion at the Probation Office and once at the home of his co-defendant.

I have read the CPS documentation in these cases and I have interviewed J's partner and co-defendant and written the PSR in her case.

The offences

1. The first in this series of offences is that of theft of a television from a catalogue company which took place between December 1991 and January 1992. In order to carry out the theft, J ordered a television from a mail order firm in another person's name. When the television was delivered, J intercepted it, saying that he would take it in for the other person and return it to her later. He did not return the television but sold it

using the money, he claims, for his and [partner's] children's Christmas presents. He says that he decided to commit this crime because he was short of money with which to finance an adequate Christmas.

2. Two cases of deception and one of attempted deception on ... These are cases where J and his co-defendant . . . used a stolen Barclaycard that they had been given. J tells me that the goods, music cassette tapes, videos and clothing, were for his own and his family's use. His motivation was, he says, lack of money to obtain these goods legitimately. I understand these goods were passed to someone else and were not recovered.

3. Theft of coal . . . J tells me that he went to a nearby pit in order to obtain one bag of coal for use in his own home. He says that he did not have the money to buy a bag and needed to keep the fire going.

4. Theft from . . . on . . . This was a case of shoplifting; J says that he and [partner] did not have enough money to sustain his family and thus they stole food and items for their own use. The reason they were without funds was because they had been burgled, and everything, including food, had been taken. The Department of Social Security had apparently refused an immediate crisis loan.

In all of these cases, then, J maintains he was motivated solely by a desire to provide a standard of living for himself, his partner and their children that was not possible on the level of benefit which the family was receiving.

My assessment, given J's explanation and the fact that he has no previous history of this type of dishonesty, is that towards the end of 1991 and at points during 1992 J seems to have come to the conclusion that the only practical solution to meeting his family's needs given, as he saw it, the inadequacy of his benefit and the impossibility of securing paid employment, was to take the risk of committing acts of dishonesty. He is forthright about the choices which he felt he faced, and offers no excuse.

Other relevant information concerning J

J lives with [partner] some of the time, but spends some nights each week at his father's address. He and [partner] have a two-year-old daughter but J claims Income Support for

104

*himself only, leaving [partner] to claim for the child. J
receives the . . . single person's allowance each week, . . . of
which he pays for board. The remaining . . . is spent on
clothes, additional food and travel about the town. J has an
outstanding Council Tax bill but as yet has made no contribution to this. He has had casual work in the . . . trade, his last
employment was two years ago. J feels that it is extremely
difficult to obtain regular work in that trade "on the books"
and that, at present, only jobs in the "unofficial" economy are
available at a wage of £1.50 (casual) per hour. He is not
prepared to take such work and thus, at present, he sees no
prospect of employment.*

Conclusions and Proposal

*The property which is the subject of these charges was
recovered with the exception of the most valuable item, the
television set. Compensation may be required in respect of
that item and those obtained via the Barclaycard and the
requirement to make this financial recompense may be taken
into account in the decision as to sentence. Factors which
may be seen to aggravate the seriousness of these offences are,
I feel, the calculated nature of the television theft, and the commission of additional, although smaller, thefts whilst on bail.
There are, though, no previous convictions that have relevance
and the situation appears to be that J has only adopted
dishonesty as a means of resolving his problems relatively
recently. He is, I feel, quite angry about his situation - that is
his lack of any prospect of betterment and his tendency to be
within an economic group that can be subject to exploitation.
It is in the context of these feelings, and, of course, within the
context of his relationship with his partner, that he has made
the decision to commit these offences.
Given that these are offences against property and, in terms
of their value and threat to the community, they are at the
lesser end of the scale, I suggest that they can be viewed as
being serious enough to attract a community penalty but not a
term of imprisonment. Though J is capable of performing
Community Service work he has said, quite honestly, that he
does not feel able to give his consent to performing unpaid
work. I recognise that the court may not view this attitude very
favourably but I would say that, in itself, is one illustration of
J's current view of the world - the view that has helped to lead
him to come into conflict with the law.*

Irrespective of J's view of Community Service, my proposal to the court would be for a Probation Order of twelve months duration. The Probation Order would be administered with stringent reporting requirements and breach would inevitably results [sic] from non-compliance. Within supervision I feel that there is a possibility that J's energies and possible resourcefulness could be redirected. Specifically it would be the aim of the order to:

1. Raise the issue of "victims" of crime - at present J does not seem to recognise that there are direct and indirect victims of his criminal activity;

2. Examine the possibilities of job training or education in order that J can escape the ranks of those who, he feels, are ripe for exploitation by others;

3. Look at money organisation, having realistic expectations and living lawfully within a budget.

I do feel that these are realistic, achievable and worthwhile aims and I believe that it is worth attempting to redirect J in this way, particularly since imprisonment will, almost certainly, result in confirming him in more hardened views on criminality.

For these reasons I would proffer the proposal of a Probation Order, bearing in mind, also, the financial recompense to be made to the ... Catalogue Company and Barclaycard. J said that he understands the conditions to which he would be subject under terms of Probation supervision and has told me that he would give his consent to the making of such an Order.

These two reports are those which most closely matched national standards within their group and, in so far as national standards are agreed to promote competent practice, may therefore be regarded as "good" reports. However, one way in which the two differ is that, unlike the social inquiry report author, the pre-sentence report author not only describes the offence but gives her/his own explicit assessment of the offender's motivation and of the aggravating and mitigating circumstance as required by national standards. We would argue that this produces a more competent report in that the evidence of careful assessment contributes to the logic behind the argument for probation rather than community service.

Conclusion

In our discussion of probation values, we have ignored a number of difficult questions raised by the topic and, although we cannot begin to attempt answers here, some of those questions must be noted. Perhaps the most obvious one is whether moral values as broad as "respect for persons" and "justice" are of any use operationally. Such values are far from unique to probation officers or social workers and almost everyone would say they believe in justice but there is considerable scope for disagreement about what is just or unjust. We noted earlier that it was difficult to distinguish in practice between the different kinds of beliefs which make up valuations; ideas about justice are interwoven with social beliefs about the 'good' society. Another operational difficulty is that moral values may sometimes be in conflict and judgments have to be made about which should take priority.

Another question which needs answering is how competence in probation practice is to be defined. It is important to recognise that what is regarded as good professional practice has changed and will change over time. Twenty or thirty years ago, reports loaded with details of the defendant's developmental history and family background, containing what would now be regarded as moralistic, sexist and racist comments, were nevertheless seen as "good" reports.

Whilst there are many ambiguities still surrounding the notion of probation values, it may be said with some certainty that behind national standards are changes in government thinking about the role of the probation service which may not only change professional values but also bring conflict for many probation officers because they do not share the new values. In the title of this chapter we ask who calls the tune. If values change over time, who decides what those values should be - the pipers or those who pay the pipers? If a democratically elected government requires the probation service to change to become an agency supervising punishment in the community and to make the consequent adjustments to the service's professional values, what gives probation officers the right to resist because they do not share the new values? These are uncomfortable questions which probation officers may be forced to face and to which they will need to have clear answers formulated if their moral values are to continue to be represented in our penal system.

Unfortunately, attempts over the last few years to adapt to changes in government policy have not been based on an understanding of the common thread running through the history of the probation service but on a pragmatic response to an increasingly unsympathetic environment. The result is that there is an uncertainty in the service about what is its special contribution to the criminal justice process. To conclude this chapter, therefore, we shall outline what, in our view, is the unique contribution the probation service makes to the criminal justice process. We argue that this lost vision has to be recaptured if probation moral values are to survive.

The story of the "death of the rehabilitative ideal" in probation has been told many times but it bears repeating in this context. We believe that the threat to traditional probation values is not a new one but began in the fifties and sixties, when a deterministic approach to offending replaced the earlier belief that people had some choice about whether or not they offended. Crime was regarded as the result of individual pathology and "treatment" in the form of casework was provided to "cure" offenders of committing crime. That deterministic approach meant that evidence of willingness on the part of the offender to stop offending was not seen as necessary to success. Success was the natural consequence of the skilled attentions of the probation officer *qua* therapist.

That approach did not prove to be very effective with the majority of offenders and in the mid-seventies there was much talk of the "death of the rehabilitative ideal". The head of the Home Office Research and Planning Unit, John Croft (Croft, 1978), hinted that unless probation officers found new, more effective ways of dealing with offenders, they might lose their jobs. However, it can be argued that what replaced the discredited psychological determinism was sociological determinism - the idea that crime was caused by social conditions. Probation officers began concentrating on helping offenders with their welfare needs (sometimes to the exclusion of any discussion of the person's attitude to offending).

As with treatment, probation officers did not regard willingness to reform as a necessary pre-condition for recommending an order. Being at risk of custody was the criterion used. Not surprisingly, the government, concerned with cost effectiveness, has not seen helping offenders with their welfare needs independent of a connection with offending behaviour as a viable alternative to the devalued treatment approach. Their solution was to attempt to persuade sentencers that probation supervision was a community punishment. That some probation managers too have accepted the language of punishment (see for example King, 1994) could be seen as the final betrayal of probation moral values; but that is to fail to recognise that neither the treatment nor the welfare approach was compatible with them either since they were based on the assumption that offenders cannot help offending. Clearly, whether or not someone offends is likely to be influenced by their social conditions, upbringing and personality. Offenders' choices are often heavily constrained. But to regard them as having no choice at all and to be totally at the mercy of nature and nurture fits oddly with such tenets of social work as the intrinsic value of people and their innate capacity to change.

Sentencers, though, appear to have retained an understanding of the special role of the probation service, failing to respond either to the idea that probation orders should be made simply because of an offender's social circumstances or that probation is intended as a punishment. Their task is to choose whether to look back to the offence and punish the offender for committing it, or to the future and how they can best ensure that s/he does not offend in future. A large proportion of the disposals available to them are primarily intended to punish offending and deter the individual and others from reoffending. Such sentences look to the past. There is another smaller group of disposals such as discharges, deferred sentences and probation orders which have traditionally looked forward and given the offender the chance to prove that s/he intends to lead a law-abiding life in future. Before choosing such a disposal, however, sentencers usually require some evidence that there is a reasonable chance of the offender being successful in keeping out of trouble. This has traditionally been sought through the medium of a probation report whose special contribution to the process is its skilled assessment of the defendant's attitude to offending and what assistance might prevent further appearances in court.

Added to this aspect of probation work is the exceptional nature of the probation order, namely, that it is the only disposal available to sentencers in the adult courts by which they can be assured that offenders will be offered skilled support and assistance in stopping offending. Its unique feature lies in the fact that every probation order should be different, distinctive and tailored to the particular individual who is its object.

Sadly the service appears to have lost confidence in (or forgotten) the value of this contribution, failing to recognise its importance and singularity in the penal system.

Certainly, there is nothing new or startling in this characterisation of the contribution of probation service to the criminal justice process. However, in a phrase used by an anthropologist (Kluckhohn 1965) to illustrate the value of an outsider looking at an unfamiliar culture, it would not be a fish which discovered the existence of water. Perhaps in the same way, probation officers at all grades are so immersed in their organisation that they sometimes fail to see and promote the service's enduring benefit to the effective operation of criminal justice and the values on which its contribution relies. Yet it may be that only by doing so will these values be retained.

Paradoxically, national standards for pre-sentence reports may contribute to the process. We saw in the comparison of pre-sentence and social inquiry reports that the former are more likely to contain a careful assessment of the defendant's offending behaviour. If as a result of compliance with national standards, reports more often contain a skilled assessment, the confidence of the courts in the ability of the service to offer skilled assistance to offenders to stop offending may thereby be increased. Sentencers could then be a powerful ally in promoting probation as an expression of the faith in the capacity of people to change and grow.

References

Boswell, G. & Worthing, M. "Reflecting Probation Service Values in Management", *Probation Journal*, 35, 1988; 128-130

Bottoms & Stelman, *Social Inquiry Reports: a framework for practice development*, Aldershot, Wildwood House, 1988

Celnick, A. "SIR to PSR: same difference?" South Yorkshire Probation Service Research Unit, 1994

Celnick, M. A. "Social work help in probation practice: an exploration of some issues raised by the experience of a special probation project team", University of Sheffield, unpublished doctoral thesis, 1989

Cochrane, D., Pratt, D. & Winter, R. K. "Who Sets the Scene for Seriousness?", *Probation Journal*, 40, 1993; 9-13

Croft, J. *Research in Criminal Justice*, Home Office Research Study No. 44, HMSO, 1978

Davies, M. The Essential Social Worker, Heinemann, 1981

Drakeford, M. "Privatisation, Punishment and the Future for Probation", *Probation Journal*, 35, 1988; 43-47

Duff, R. A. *Trials and Punishments*, Cambridge, Cambridge University Press, 1986

Garland, D. *Punishment and Modern Society: A Study in Modern Society*, Oxford, Clarendon, 1991

Harris, R. "Probation Officers: Still Social Workers?" *Probation Journal*, 36, 1989; 52-57

Home Office, *Social Inquiry Reports: General Guidance on Contents*, Home Office Circular 17/1983: Home Office, 1983

Home Office, *Social Inquiry Reports, Home Office Circular* 92/1986: Home Office, 1986

Home Office, *National Standards for the Supervision of Offenders in the Community*, HMSO, 1992

Home Office and Lord Chancellor's Office, *Report of the Interdepartmental Committee on the Business of the Criminal Courts*, HMSO, 1961

Home Office Inspectorate of Probation, *The Criminal Justice Act 1991 Inspection*, Home Office, 1993

Howe, D. "Agency Function and social work principles", *British Journal of Social Work*, 9 (2), 1979

Hudson, B. *Justice through Punishment: A Critique of the "Justice" Model of Corrections*, Macmillan, 1987

Kemshall, H. "Quality: Friend or Foe", *Probation Journal*, 40, 1993; 123-126

King, R. Probation: a different kind of punishment", *Justice of the Peace*, 158, 1994; 322-3

Kluckhohn, C. Mirror for Man, New York, Fawcett Publications, 1965

McWilliams, W. "The English Social Enquiry Report: Development and Practice", University of Sheffield unpublished doctoral thesis, 1986

Schofield, H. "NAPO and the Criminal Justice Act", *NAPO News*, February 1992; no.37, 3

Weston, W. R. "Probation in penal philosophy: evolutionary per-spective", *Howard Journal*, 17, 1978; 7-22

SIX: PROBATION VALUES IN WORK WITH PRISONERS

Brian Williams

Although throughcare work is in some ways no different from any other kind of probation work, it tests individual workers' commitment to professional values more severely than supervision of clients in the community. It brings probation officers and social workers face to face with prisons and their staff, and this raises issues about confidentiality and trust, as well as the more obvious questions of how to deliver a personal service to clients trapped in a large and impersonal total institution. It involves assessment of risk to the public, and this process brings issues of care, control and opposition to custodial solutions to offending into sharp relief.

Just as a society's treatment of its prisoners might be taken as a measure of its degree of civilisation, probation officers' commitment to implementing their values where imprisoned clients are concerned is perhaps an accurate indicator of their ability to put such values into practice at all. (Not that individual probation officers can take all the credit or blame: even to attempt this requires a prior commitment of resources including time, and a willingness within organisations to legitimate the practitioners' concern. These issues will be discussed at greater length towards the end of this chapter).

WHAT VALUES?

As suggested in the Introduction, it is impossible to assume that there is a codified and agreed set of principles or values common to probation officers, and there is a habit of referring rather loosely to 'probation values' as if their exact nature was self-evident. The values identified in that discussion are undoubtedly among those on which probation work is based, however, and in this chapter it will be argued that they stand the test of being applied to practice.

Different areas of practice test workers' principles in varying ways. In the discussion that follows, it should become clear that the general principles identified in the Introduction remain valid where a particular area of practice is involved. The discussion will therefore assume that the values underpinning probation work with prisoners are the same as, or similar to, the ones already identified, namely:

- opposition to custody, and a commitment to constructive ways of dealing with offenders;
- commitment to equality of opportunity and to justice;

113

- protecting clients' right to confidentiality (subject to explicit constraints) and promoting openness about processes and decisions affecting them;

- valuing and accepting clients as unique and self-determined individuals, keeping this separate from the "confronting" of offending behaviour;

- protecting victims and potential victims of crime, keeping this apart from meeting offenders' needs where appropriate;

- promoting positive change through the use of professional relationships.

Each of these basic principles is problematic in practice, and it is when we come to consider some of the contradictions inherent in social work values, and some of the particular difficulties thrown up to test them in day-to-day work with prisoners, that these strains become apparent. It is important to expose such problems, because the values are strengthened if they can withstand such a test, and they need reconsidering if they cannot.

Some of the generic probation values are also applied rather differently where work with prisoners is concerned, as we shall see in what follows. For example, the commitment to work with offenders in constructive ways and to avoid the unnecessary recourse to imprisonment has either failed or been rejected by sentencers in the case of probation clients in prison. This does not mean that the basic value position has no relevance to this area of work, because it should inform the ways in which probation officers work with prisoners. Similarly, the probation officer's role as mediator between the client and the system takes on a new aspect when dealing with prisons.

APPLYING PROBATION VALUES
WHEN WORKING WITH PRISONERS

OPPOSITION TO CUSTODY AND COMMITMENT TO CONSTRUCTIVE WAYS OF DEALING WITH OFFENDERS

Most probation staff and criminologists view imprisonment as destructive and unnecessary for the majority of people who are imprisoned in the UK today. Taking that as read, what does it mean to maintain this anti-custodial stance when working with clients who have actually been imprisoned?

It has been argued that generic social work training has obscured some of the values issues which trainee probation officers should be encouraged to confront, and that a new value base specific to probation is needed, giving centrality to anti-custodialism, restorative justice and community safety (Nellis, forthcoming). It does seem that opposition to the prodigal use of imprisonment has been rather muted on the part of the probation service in the face of recent political commitment to increasing it, and it may be that those of us who train probation officers have to take part of the responsibility for this. The credibility of the probation service with prisoners would be increased by more effective campaigning against the increasing over-use of imprisonment, but the service has been more concerned in recent years to resist the attacks on its own credibility mounted by the very proponents of the "prison works" philosophy.

The evidence is that prison does not "work" as intended (Raynor, et al, 1994; Hudson, 1993; Mathiesen, 1990) - if we take the intention to be the prevention of further offending rather than the pathologising of delinquents (Foucault, 1977; Howe, 1994). In a few cases, it may have incidental benefits, and in some others it may be influential in changing offenders' behaviour. Overall, however, it works to prevent reoffending in fewer cases than any other disposal. It may be inevitable in some cases, but it is often damaging and unnecessary. It seems to me that a particular aspect of the basic social work value of affirming clients' individuality arises from this understanding. If we know that prison is unnecessary and likely to be damaging in a particular case, do we make it clear to the client that we understand this?

The objection might be raised that it would threaten good order and discipline in prisons if probation officers were to go about declaring that inmates should not be there. This argument is difficult to sustain when actual cases are considered. Probation officers were among those who declared the innocence of the victims of some of the famous miscarriages of justice in the 1980s. Probation officers (and indeed prison officers) have helped to expose the high percentage of prisoners who should be in hospital or serving non-custodial sentences. Until the early 1990s even Home Office ministers urged that prison be used more sparingly, at least implying that some people were being imprisoned unnecessarily (see Home Office, 1991; Tumim et al, 1993). In the face of such obvious contradictions, the probation role in prisons must surely include a genuine and consistent opposition to the misuse of custody

Probation officers have few opportunities to campaign on general issues as part of their work (although they should also be taking such issues up through their professional associations and through penal reform groups and with influential individuals in their own time if they are committed to probation values). What they do have the opportunity to do is to act genuinely with individual clients. Surely this implies an acknowledgement of the harsh sentencing climate and the unnecessary use of custody, as it affects individuals.

If the anti-custodial stance of the probation service means anything in work with prisoners, it must be practised when working with individuals and groups. We should acknowledge the injustices of the sentencing system, and become actively involved in promoting bail schemes in remand prisons[1], in supporting prisoners in their appeals, and in promoting anti-discriminatory work. We should also be collecting the evidence the campaigning groups need to publicise abuses and over-reliance on custody. In many cases, the support of the prison service will be readily forthcoming: people with mental illnesses, for example, are hard to cope with in over-crowded prisons, as are very young offenders and many deportees. The Home Office itself has recently made it clear that another difficult group, those who refuse to admit their guilt, are not excluded from parole (although it is made clear, without apparent intentional irony, that this applies only as long as they consent to discuss their offending behaviour), and this presents new opportunities and challenges for individual work by probation officers in conjunction with prison staff.

Even where we can do nothing to help get people out of prison, we do not need to collude with unnecessary imprisonment by refusing to comment on it during interviews or groupwork. It is likely, in many cases, to help build up a constructive relationship if we agree that imprisonment has been used inappropriately.

The anti-custodial ethos will also influence probation officers' approach to work with clients and colleagues in prison. There is an increasing emphasis on liaison between field probation officers and both prison-based probation staff and prison officers. In many cases this will clearly be in prisoners' interests, for example in the process of compiling sentence plans (where these are actually being done, which still seems to be rather hit-or-miss), or in making a case for bail through a prison's bail information scheme. It is important, however, that probation officers do not become habituated to liaising and sharing information about clients without their explicit consent. We shall return to this issue below in the discussion of confidentiality.

Clearly, probation officers in and outside prisons need to cultivate professional working relationships with prison staff.

The anti-custodial values of the service do have implications, though, for such links. Like psychologists or chaplains, probation officers take their value-base into prisons with them. Prison-based staff can therefore be expected to take the lead in some of the types of initiative described above (and have regularly done so). Field probation officers represent an important link with the outside community for prisoners, and they may need to be prepared to articulate the anti-custodial ethos when liaising with prisons on clients' behalf. For example, probation officers may appropriately become involved in defending the rights of deportees, or in supporting prisoners who complain of discriminatory treatment. To do so, they need to be familiar with the relevant precedents and rules, and to be prepared to stand partly outside the system whilst remaining involved in it. This is one of the most difficult aspects of the role, but a crucial one at times.

On a more mundane level, the anti-custodial stance involves expecting professionalism of prison staff and being prepared to confront unacceptable attitudes and behaviour towards clients. The prisons' race relations policy, for example, sets a high standard which will only be met in practice if those from outside who have access to the prisons are vigilant and involved in monitoring its delivery (Kett *et al*, 1992; Williams, forthcoming). Similarly, if probation officers are to put their proverbial money where their mouth is, their own practice needs to be especially professional where throughcare is concerned. It is so easy to lose sight of the needs of imprisoned clients; they do not usually make many demands, they do not often turn up at the office unexpectedly, many do not write or phone, and their families often have no idea what help the probation service could offer.

This implies that field probation officers should reach out to imprisoned clients and their families to make clear what service is on offer. This, it could be argued, is part of the operationalisation of the anti-custodial stance. If probation officers are meant to be the humane part of the penal system, many prisoners might ask, where are they when we need their help?[2]

OPPOSING DISCRIMINATION AND PROMOTING JUSTICE

A number of recent publications explore what it means to practice anti-oppressively in throughcare work (Kett et al, 1992; Eaton, 1993; Preece, 1993; Player, 1994; Dominelli *et al*, forthcoming). The present writer has also examined elsewhere the notion of promoting justice in throughcare (Williams, 1994) and what follows will not repeat the arguments made in this material.

Instead, this section will concentrate on the resources available for practitioners committed to anti-oppressive practice.

The probation service has a unique and important position when it comes to arguing for justice in the administration of the criminal justice system. Service organisations, managers and probation practitioners are well placed to influence the ways in which the system operates and in which individual offenders are treated. The officially legitimated role of the probation service includes mediating and negotiating on offenders' behalf with other agencies, and in some respects probation is in a powerful position to help to bring those other agencies together to explore value conflicts and to consider the interests of individual clients.

As Anne Worrall notes in her chapter in this volume, justice is a slippery concept, and one that can be interpreted narrowly or more broadly. The probation service has always been concerned with promoting the broader definition: justice is not just about procedural rights, it involves attention to client need and to inequalities.

The extent to which the different "players" have actually sought to exploit the pivotal role of probation varies. The service organisations are all involved in promoting equality of opportunity, although the depth of their commitment is not uniform. The employers, through the Central Probation Council (CPC, formerly the Central Council of Probation Committees), responded to events in the 1980s but also tried to stimulate members of the then probation committees to take a wider view of their role in speaking up for underprivileged clients and communities. It appears that the CPC was rather more radical in its view of these matters than the local committees were prepared to be (Holdaway & Mantle, 1992), but attempts to move thinking forward have continued, concentrating on helping local services to develop coherent and effective policies on race issues but also looking at gender and poverty, and developing training for magistrates as well as for probation staff. The tendency of magistrates to individualise offending, reinforced by the way the system in this country is organised, has hampered such developments: if they believe that each case in court is sentenced on its individual merits, it is hard for magistrates to believe simultaneously that sentencing is characterised by institutional racism and sexism.

The professional association representing chief officer grades, the Association of Chief Officers of Probation (ACOP), has also been actively involved in promoting equality of opportunity, both through policy formulation and (from the late 1980s) by contributions to public debate. Much of ACOP's policy material is potentially very helpful to practitioners[3], but it is not always effectively distributed or promoted.

Local probation service management has moved the debate on

anti-oppressive practice forward, too, although it is framed at this level in terms of "equal opportunities". While services' equal opportunities policies are often bland and highly general (or so detailed as to be impenetrably bureaucratic), they have undoubtedly changed the climate experienced by staff, at least to some extent. Obvious forms of discrimination such as race and to a lesser extent gender have been highlighted, but issues relating to (for example) disability and heterosexism have been played down by many services. This reflects political realities: the utterances of ministers have discouraged chief officers from explicit statements that such forms of oppression will be challenged.

The best such policies, however, are powerful statements of principle which can be empowering for staff keen to promote professional values, and some are reasonably specific about the implications for work in particular areas like throughcare: see for example Avon Probation Service, 1992; South Yorkshire PS, 1993; Essex PS, 1994; Kett *et al*, 1992. Many such policies are generated by working parties which include specialist practitioners, giving their prescriptions greater immediacy and credibility than abstract statements devised by senior managers.

Much of the most progressive thinking on these issues has been undertaken by the probation officers' trade union, NAPO - encouraged and kept on its toes by the Association of Black Probation Officers (ABPO). The involvement of NAPO predates that of the other organisations, and there is less reluctance to engage with unpopular causes - although the extent to which NAPO's policies are implemented depends on their "ownership" by a diverse membership. It is when NAPO takes controversial positions that the debate moves forward, however painful this process might be at times (as, for example, in the NAPO-inspired debate about whether probation officers should work in prisons at all - or, more recently, NAPO's initiative in demanding anti-sexism training for prison staff).

NAPO's publications are readily available to main grade staff and students, as is the opportunity to participate in its work, and in this it seems less remote than the other organisations. Its campaigning activities are also open to practitioners, although its head office staff do much of the work of attending meetings and drafting documents. There are few fields of anti-oppressive practice on which it has not worked, and in many there are detailed practice guidelines. A particularly useful model for practitioners is provided by the "manifesto for action" approach adopted in ensuring the implementation of NAPO's anti-racist policies. The document (NAPO, 1991) encourages work at team level to educate staff and to act on

119

evidence of discrimination, although it now needs updating again.

ABPO, which began as a campaigning group and a forum for support for the few black staff then working in the probation service, has concentrated on these roles and more recently on consultation at national level with the other interest groups and the Home Office. It has been highly effective, but has not devoted its energies to producing many publications for general use. Similar comments apply to the smaller LAGIP (Lesbians and Gays in Probation).

There are, however, plenty of policies and guidelines for probation workers committed to anti-oppressive work to use. Many of them restate a simple truth: anti-discriminatory practice is good practice. There may be a need for knowledge as well as commitment, and sometimes relevant training is hard to obtain. There is usually a need for mutual support, and services have begun to recognise this, for example by allowing ABPO and NAPO members to devote paid time to their work within the associations (although this is not always the case).

The larger penal reform groups (particularly NACRO and the Prison Reform Trust) have sponsored and published a good deal of research into discrimination in the criminal justice system and into ways of combating it (Alfred, 1992; NACRO, 1991, 1992; Shaw, 1993; Worrall, 1994).

Anti-discriminatory practice in the prison setting is challenging, as it is elsewhere. It may be that **anti-oppressive** practice in its true meaning is impossible in the prison setting, which is by definition an oppressive place to be, but that does not excuse probation workers' evasion of their obligations. Although uniformed staff are often stereotyped by probation officers, their occupational culture is strong and in many ways destructive. One aspect of this is the prevalence of racist and sexist attitudes, often unashamedly expressed (Sim, 1994; Genders & Player, 1989; Hercules, 1989; McDermott, 1990; Alfred, 1992; Fletcher, 1988; NAPO, 1987; NAPO, 1991). While it is imperative to challenge this, it can sap the energies of prison-based probation staff to do so constantly, and many adopt strategies to protect themselves from burn-out and from constant confrontation.

There has been a tendency to regard the dominant culture of prisons as unassailable, or even to suggest that it is somehow impolite to challenge it (the view questioned by Kett *et al*, that "we are part of someone else's institution and have no right to interfere' (1992: 52). As they say, this attitude will no longer do, and the prison service's race relations policy contradicts it). What many prison-based probation staff are now doing is to form alliances with prison staff who have committed themselves to equality and to reform. Sometimes this is in terms of personal support to women and black workers; often it involves joining uniformed and management staff in setting up initiatives and in working to support race relations liaison officers in the implementation of prison service policies.

For white field probation officers working with black prisoners, there is a good deal of scope to involve groups from black communities. Apart from the national organisations there are now such groups in many cities (such as the Black Justice Project in Sheffield and Nottingham Black Initiative), and some services employ black outreach workers to ensure that black prisoners receive a proper throughcare service (as in South Yorkshire).

Anti-discriminatory throughcare work also needs to involve more purposeful and systematic work with foreign prisoners. One or two services, most notably Middlesex, have begun to make progress on this issue (Cheney, 1994; Dominelli *et al*, forthcoming).

The service needs to do more to support women working in and with prisons: only recently has the destructive and wearing nature of sexist remarks and behaviour been acknowledged. Individual staff can contribute to this support, but a strategy for managing the problem is needed.

CONFIDENTIALITY AND OPENNESS

It is clear that confidentiality is difficult to maintain in prison work, and that as a value supposedly central to social work, it has been much abused. The related idea that clients have a right to know what is being written about them and what decisions are being made is also difficult to implement when working with prisoners, although the climate has recently become more favourable.

It might be argued that the probation service can take little credit for this: most improvements in the situation regarding prisoners' access to information have arisen from litigation, although ACOP put a good deal of work into securing the national throughcare framework (Prison Service, 1994). This document does implicitly support greater openness, but has little to say about prisoners' right to participate in the planning of their sentences. One role for probation staff in prisons is to press for the fulfilment of the promise of openness: there can be no justification for waiting until prisoners' rights are gradually opened up by European Court judgments. As in other areas, though, there is a need for realism about the extent to which probation departments can influence prison policy: their position is marginal (Walker & Beaumont, 1981; Williams, 1992a; Roberts, 1994) and their influence limited.

Confidentiality as a value has been central to social and probation work ever since the value base began to be formalised (see Introduction). It is closely linked with the idea that relationships between professionals and their clients depend upon trust, and thus with the value of respect for persons (Butrym, 1976). It is a central value, and the priority accorded to it tells us much about the profession's degree of respect for its clients.

When David Brandon experimented in the 1970s, he found that probation officers were frequently willing to give out personal information about clients by phone without checking the caller's identity (Brandon, 1975). It would be interesting to repeat the experiment now. Prison probation officers are probably more aware of the dangers than they once were, not least because of the liberties taken by "investigative" journalists, and perhaps there is greater professionalism about this issue generally. The real problem as some prisoners see it is that the professional community within which confidences belong has expanded to include prison officers working alongside probation staff. In many areas of work, inter-agency partnerships expand the network further (Thomas, 1988).

Some field probation staff used confidentiality as their justification for not giving information about clients' bail applications to uniformed prison staff during NAPO's industrial action against bail information schemes in the early 1990s, although there was a wide-spread belief that this was not the real reason (Williams, 1992). In that case, clients had generally given written permission for information to be shared, and in that sense it was a highly unusual situation. What is much more common is for probation reports in prison files, and probation files in prisons with shared working schemes, to be open to prison staff. It is unclear to what extent this is made known to clients, but many prisoners resent prison officers' detailed knowledge of their personal circumstances (Williams, 1992a). There is a lack of clarity - and indeed of policy - about the basis on which confidential information about clients is shared at present. The information is seen as belonging to the prison rather than to the probation service or indeed the client. This gives rise to situations which compromise the values of the probation service, and is a key example of the difficulties of working in a "host" organisation with its own, very different, values.

It is perhaps unfair to expect prison officers, whose training in such matters is very limited, to appreciate the professional commitment to confidentiality or why it is so important to clients. Where probation officers have a training role, this is clearly an area which should be given a high priority. If successful and routine shared working is ever to become a reality in most prisons, uniformed staff need access to far more training, covering the values of the caring professions among other things. As it is, prison probation departments involved in shared working schemes routinely share confidential client information with prison officers whose perceptions of how it is appropriate to use such material may differ significantly from those of the staff who collected the information from clients and others on the basis of confidentiality.

The policy discussed in Una Padel's chapter in this book demonstrates the kind of dilemmas arising from the present situation: how can ACOP's and NAPO's positions on respecting confidentiality with reference to HIV status be implemented in the prison setting? As the author of the ACOP paper noted, taken-for-granted probation attitudes to confidentiality are severely tested by HIV and AIDS (ACOP, 1990). This is perhaps one instance where the probation service's clarity about clients' right to respect for confidentiality had some influence: the collusion of the prison medical service with unprofessional practices such as segregation of HIV+ prisoners was exposed by the Woolf report and, earlier, by prison reform groups including NAPO (Fletcher, 1990; Thomas, 1990; Thomas & Costigan, 1992; NAPO, 1992).

The current situation of newly imprisoned people with HIV/AIDS is very much better as a result (Ralli, 1994), and some agreement about proper professional practice on confidentiality has finally emerged. Having achieved this much, the probation service may have to accept that its trust has nevertheless been forfeited in the eyes of many HIV+ prisoners, and hand AIDS counselling in prisons over to others who are better qualified to provide it (Williams, 1995).

There are clearly limits upon the duty to protect the confidentiality of information disclosed by clients, and again, the prison setting throws this issue into sharp relief. Most prison-based probation staff are acutely aware of uniformed staff expectations that loyalty to them will outweigh loyalty to clients. In most cases this is unlikely to be problematic: if a prisoner is lighting fires, for example, others may deliberately drop hints to probation officers as to the fire-raiser's identity in an attempt to protect their own safety. In this situation, it is not for probation officers to protect the information or to make judgements about its reliability. Similar considerations apply in the case of information which comes to probation officers' attention concerning bullying and harassment among inmates. Unfortunately, few of the conflicts about confidentiality are so easy to resolve.

Probation officers interacting with security-conscious prison staff have to bear in mind the ways in which client information may be interpreted. Field probation workers may at first be surprised by the ways in which information about their clients is reframed at meetings with prison staff. Such differences of interpretation can be crucial when parole decisions are being made, and at times it may be necessary to have reports checked by experienced prison-based colleagues with this in mind. These considerations apply to all multidisciplinary working situations, of course. It is significant that ACOP and NAPO have different policies on whether to record clients' HIV status: attitudes to the importance of confidentiality can vary according to workers' status as well as their agencies.

Returning to the issue of openness, it can be important to ensure that clients are aware of the limits of confidentiality. This needs to be on the agenda from the beginning of probation contact with them: for example, the subject of a PSR needs to know that it will go with them if they are imprisoned, and that its contents are available to prison officers, psychologists, and to those considering allocation and early release. Such warnings might reduce the flow of information, but in my experience they also improve trust. Clarity from an early stage about the practical ownership of information is likely to make it easier to discuss such issues in future: for example, when explaining to a Schedule One offender that the police will be informed by the field probation officer of his movements after release.

Confidentiality, then, is an issue for explicit discussion with clients - in throughcare work as in other contexts. The constraints upon probation staff in their attempts to protect private information need to be acknowledged openly. The situations in which other considerations override the general commitment to confidentiality can also profitably be discussed. The issues are by no means clear-cut, but client involvement may often clarify them.

VALUING AND ACCEPTING CLIENTS

It may seem self-evident that the fundamental values underlying probation work include acceptance of clients as unique and self-determined individuals. To ask ourselves how to implement this in total institutions such as prisons, and how to value and accept people who have committed sometimes appalling offences, does raise ethical as well as practical issues. Much of the literature on social work values, while acknowledging the difficulty of putting client self-determination and non-judgmentalism into practice, fails to give examples of how it might be done or of the kinds of behaviour which might simultaneously need to be confronted.

Parsloe, for example, blithely asserts: "With time and a knowledge of human growth in general and this human's development in particular, the officer can usually come to feel acceptance without judgement for most clients." (Parsloe, 1967, 88-9). She also implicitly refers back to the police court missionaries' formula, "love the sinner, hate the sin". How, then, do probation officers who are the parents of young children go about working in an accepting and non-judgemental way with persistent, unrepentant, repeatedly imprisoned child-abusers, allowing them individual self-determination?

To pose the question so baldly is, of course, to over-simplify the issues. Using this example, however, let us separate and clarify some of them.

It has been pointed out elsewhere that self-determination assumes that clients are free to make choices, and that the very concept acts as a smokescreen to obscure the real limitations upon such choice (Rojek, 1989; Corrigan & Leonard, 1978). In work with serious offenders, the notion of self-determination has recently been reframed by "just deserts" theorists. One of their arguments is that punishment should be proportionate and rationed: it should be imposed only to the extent that it is necessary and effective (Hudson, 1993). While this supports the idea of offenders as self-determined, it rather redefines it. Individual offenders have little choice about which punishment is regarded as proportionate in their cases, but "deserts" theories regard them as self-determined in the sense that doing the crime leads logically to doing the time. "Just deserts" theorists see offending purely as an individual decision, completely denying the importance of social factors (Raynor *et al*, 1994). This line of thinking ignores the rather obvious fact that "although people choose to act, sometimes criminally, they do not do so under conditions of their own choosing" (Box, 1987, 29).

This does not release probation officers from the ethical obligation to attempt an accepting and helping relationship with serious offenders. It will, however, be easier in some cases than in others. Offenders who have repeatedly taken advantage of power over vulnerable victims, and who see nothing wrong in this, are unpromising material for offending behaviour work. The temptation is to supervise such clients in a routine, undemanding way, requiring minimum compliance with national standards without any real engagement. There is some evidence that the prison service has set up its Sex Offender Treatment Programme in just such a mechanistic way, ignoring the profound personal issues such work arouses

(Waite, 1994). Yet it might be argued that such difficult (albeit often superficially deferential and compliant) clients are the ones on whom probation officers should be concentrating their attention (see Bryan Gocke's chapter in the present volume).

One of the criticisms emerging from consumer research into probation work with prisoners is that it has become bureaucratised and impersonal (Williams, 1991; 1992a; Mitchell, 1992; McAllister *et al*, 1992). At least in some cases, this arises from a reluctance to engage with people who have committed repulsive offences, partly because workers see no way to do so effectively. There is some evidence, however, that work based on clarifying offenders' moral reasoning processes can be effective in changing serious offending behaviour, and that the nature of the relationships between staff and clients is an important variable (Ross & Fabiano, 1985; Cormier, 1994). There are ethical issues about the extent to which such work is done openly: are clients being manipulated, or are they aware of the process?

In Canadian prisons, for example, moral-cognitive work was initially undertaken through the provision of higher education classes. Offending behaviour was never explicitly the focus of the classes, and prisoners would probably have steered clear of involvement if it were. Duguid, who pioneered this approach, has admitted that the subterfuge was unjustified (Williams, 1993).

Explicit and focused work on offenders' moral reasoning does, however, seem a promising way of confronting offending without denying the individual right to self-determination. What this will mean in practice has only recently begun to emerge, but early results seem encouraging (Raynor *et al*, 1994).

PROTECTING THE VICTIMS AND POTENTIAL VICTIMS OF CRIME

It is one of the central functions of social and probation work to protect victims. The reader may question whether it is appropriate, however, to elevate this to the level of a value. It seems to me that unless we do so, we relegate it to an inferior status. The protection of victims and potential victims of crime is surely an overriding value: for example, the need to protect children is often held to overrule the principle of confidentiality of client information. This principle comes into effect in work with prisoners, when the law and professional values agree that the movements of Schedule One offenders against children should be monitored after their release from prison, and what might in other circumstances be confidential information is routinely given to the police. It is important, however, to note that the promotion of the interests of victims is, wherever possible, kept separate from direct work with offenders.

This is necessary for the protection of both victims and offenders. Victims of crime were often, in the early experiments with victim-offender mediation, caused unnecessary distress by workers who contrived reparation meetings between victims and "their" offenders, and there was considerable potential for conflicts of interest. Research which evaluated some of the British experiments found that probation staff were motivated mainly by offenders' rather than by victims' needs (Davis, 1992), and that the government had a hidden agenda in promoting such projects (*ibid.*; see also Elias, 1993).

These studies deplored the "goal ambiguity" arising when victim-offender mediation was located too close to the criminal justice system (Warner, 1992: 4), and when participation by offenders was voluntary only in name. Although there was potential for setting up schemes which helped victims and also contributed to the rehabilitation of offenders, the original model used was not suitable for realising these aims. It is clearly important in principle to separate work with offenders from assistance to victims, and to do so in practice when working with individual clients and with groups.

Even where there is clarity about the need for such a separation of interests, concern for victims and potential future victims of crime can raise complex ethical dilemmas for those working with prisoners. How does a probation officer balance the interests of clients and victims?

Prison-based and home probation officers are required to discuss with certain victims and their families the implications of prisoners becoming eligible to be considered for home leave and parole. This is a highly sensitive matter, and one that has caused some difficulties since the introduction of an ill-considered clause about lifers in the Victim's Charter in 1990 (Home Office, 1990, 21; see also para 39 of the throughcare national standards: Home Office, 1992, 108-9). Some victim support schemes and probation areas are now devising ways of separating the work with victims from routine probation contact with clients as a result of lessons learned in trying to implement the Victim's Charter. Particular problems arose where the survivors of murder victims were contacted "out of the blue" by probation officers trying to comply with the recommendation on discussing victims' feelings about the possible release of lifers. Sensitively done by trained victim support workers, this might eventually prove to be a useful process, but the innovation was not based upon any research - even into victims' views in principle.

Ascertaining victims' views about the possible release of offenders from prison is something it would be difficult for probation officers to do with any degree of objectivity, and it is a task that clearly needs to be kept separate from the supervision and support of imprisoned clients. Some area services have reached agreement with local Victim Support schemes, or have established specialist units, to achieve this separation (for example, in Northumbria and West Yorkshire).

Supervision of prisoners after release is explicitly concerned with the protection of the public, according to the national standards. Although this was always the case with serious offenders on parole, it represents a change of emphasis where post-release supervision is concerned (drawing attention to the other major change embodied in the 1991 Act, whereby longer-sentence prisoners are seen as serving the non-custodial part of their sentences rather than simply being released under supervision). The provisions relating to frequency of contact and to breach are intended to highlight both public protection and the controlling aspect of supervision. While this presents probation officers with ethical difficulties, it also gives much greater priority than in the past to post-release work with longer-sentence prisoners. To this extent, it may represent an opportunity to engage more fully with ex-prisoners, at least in areas where corresponding resources are made available. This is discussed further in the next section.

The levels of contact required for post-release supervision are such that it could be done quite oppressively, and probation officers have to balance the public protection element of supervision with the need to build up a constructive relationship. When meetings are dominated by the minutiae of compliance with national standards, there is a danger that not much else gets done. The extent to which the public is really protected by weekly meetings between offenders and probation officers is not one that probation interest groups have been inclined, in the current climate of opinion, to raise with the Home Office, but there is clearly little scope for genuine control of offenders' behaviour, apart from looking out for and responding to danger signals.

As with the question of confidentiality, it is important to be open about the requirement to take victim issues into account - both for its own sake and for the sake of building a constructive relationship with the client. Ex-prisoners need to know what the agenda of supervision is and the extent to which it is predetermined by the Home Office through the national standards. Many prisoners feel quite bitter about the requirements of Schedule One registration, but they need not be explained in a bureaucratic way: in some cases, such an interview might even have some possibilities in terms of working on attitudes to offending and to victims.

PROMOTING POSITIVE CHANGE THROUGH THE USE OF PROFESSIONAL RELATIONSHIPS

It has been suggested by many of the radical writers on social and probation work that the notion of constructive professional 'relationships' between workers and clients rests upon a series of patronising and authoritarian assumptions; that the worker is morally superior to the client, and that the crime problem can be covered up by individualising it (Walker & Beaumont, 1981). In recent years, however, the rejection of 'casework' - helping people find answers to problems, many of which have structural origins but some of which are susceptible to partial solution through individual work - has gone further. The traditionally feminine, caring elements of social work have been downgraded in favour of the macho language of confronting offending and hitting management targets.

The notion of encouraging change in offenders by using professional relationships to influence them may be patronising, and it may raise questions about the appropriate balance between care and control in social work, but it is central to the social work enterprise of caring for others (Brown, 1986). It is more honest than the kind of subterfuge favoured by some of those advocating, for example, cognitive therapies (see above), and considerably more natural. Its essence is the idea that clients will take advice from people who have earned their respect, and it has its origins in explicitly religious social work. In the case of the probation service, the early police court missionaries were upstanding members of the community who aspired to lead by Christian example.

There is a valid secular equivalent today to this model of the probation officer as religious adviser. Probation officers, through their training and experience, are in a position to supervise offenders in helpful ways. They gain imprisoned clients' respect by the quality of the assistance they give them and their families. This assistance is effected through professional relationships; between probation officer, client and family, and between probation officers and other professionals. The probation officer has few resources other than the means of communication and the use of self. In that sense, it is far from outdated to think of the task of throughcare in

129

terms of purposeful, professional relationships.

In fact, given the opportunity, prisoners themselves frame their requirements of the probation service in terms of constructive relationships. They want probation officers to be clear about what they can and cannot do. During the custodial part of the sentence, they want knowledgeable, reliable, understanding, courteous and personal service from their field probation officers (Williams, 1992a).

Recent experience of cognitive skills training in Canadian prisons (where the purpose of the programmes is now made explicit to clients) suggests that its success depends upon "a relationship characterized by warmth and trust in which modelling and reinforcement can occur" (Cormier, 1994, 48). Prisoners who speak most warmly of their probation officers in this country see them either as more friends than professionals (Williams, 1992a), or more often as advocates who know their case and the system well enough to argue for early release. One said of his officer, "He goes to great pains to explain that he's trying to build up a case . . . at least he does try and encourage you that there is a chance . . . we've discussed the parole situation, and he's working towards getting me sort of 18 months, 20 months at the end of me sentence" (Williams, 1991, 85).

Even if this standard cannot always be met, throughcare ought to be able to aspire to the minimal goals outlined by Raban, "sustaining and developing community links" and "confirming the prisoner's individuality" (Raban, 1987, 95). This damage limitation model obviously involves forming constructive professional relationships with prisoners, their families, community agencies and prison staff. Relationships, after all, are what social work is all about.

[1] This is a controversial view: many in NAPO oppose bail schemes on principle. For a discussion of the arguments, see Williams (1992) and Cameron (1989).

[2] Consumer research indicates that prisoners - particularly long-termers - would welcome a more proactive approach to throughcare by field probation officers. For further reading on this issue, see Williams, 1991; Williams, 1992a; Carlen, 1990; Raban, 1987; Eaton, 1993; Liebling, 1989.

[3] See, for example, ACOP's position statements on HIV, AIDS and confidentiality (ACOP, 1990); and on the management of risk (ACOP, 1994).

References

ACOP, *Position statement on HIV, AIDS, confidentiality and the probation service,* Wakefield: ACOP, 1990

ACOP, *Guidance on management of risk and public protection,* Wakefield: ACOP, 1994

Robin, A. R. *Black workers in the prison service,* Prison Reform Trust, 1992

Box, S. *Recession, crime and punishment,* Macmillan, 1987

Brandon, D. "Clients have a right to hope for better privacy than this", *Community Care* 23 April 1975

Brown, S. "A woman's profession", in (eds.) Marchant, H. & Wearing, B. *Gender reclaimed: women in social work,* Hale & Iremonger, Sydney, 1986

Butrym, Z. T. *The nature of social work,* Macmillan, 1976

Cameron, J. "Bail schemes: the failure of reformism", *Probation Journal,* 36 (2), 1989; 78-81

Carlen, P. *Alternatives to women's imprisonment,* Milton Keynes: Open University Press, 1990

Cheney, D. "Policy and practice in work with foreign prisoners", *Probation Journal,* 41 (2), 1994; 86-91

Cormier, R. B. "Reducing re-offending: the steps Canada is taking", *Prison Service Journal,* 93, 1994; 47-50

Corrigan, P. & Leonard, P. *Social work practice under capitalism,* Macmillan, 1978

Davis, G. *Making amends: mediation and reparation in criminal justice,* Routledge, 1992

Dominelli, L., Jeffers, L., Jones, G., Sibanda, S. & Williams, B. *Anti-racist probation practice,* Aldershot: Arena, forthcoming

Eaton, M. *Women after prison,* Buckingham: Open University Press, 1993

Elias, R. *Victims still: the political manipulation of crime victims*, Sage, 1993

Fletcher, H. "Black people and the probation service", *NAPO News*, 4, 1988; 8-10

Foucault, M. *Discipline and punish*, Harmondsworth: Penguin, 1977

Genders, E. & Player, E. *Race relations in prisons*, Oxford: Clarendon, 1989

Hercules, T. *Labelled a black villain*, Fourth Estate, 1989

Holdaway, S. & Mantle, G. "Governing the probation service: probation committees and policy-making", *Howard Journal,* 31 (2), 1992; 120-32

Home Office, *Custody, care and justice*, Home Office, 1991

Home Office, *Victim's Charter*, Home Office, 1990

Home Office, *National standards for the supervision of offenders in the community*, Home Office, 1992

Howe, A. *Punish and critique: towards a feminist analysis of penality*, Routledge, 1994

Hudson, B. A. *Penal policy and social justice*, Macmillan, 1993

Kett, J. *et al, Managing and developing anti-racist practice within probation, a resource pack for action*, St Helens: Merseyside Probation Service, 1992
Liebling, A. "Temporary release: getting embroiled with prisons", *Howard Journal,* 28 (1), 1989; 51-5

Mathiesen, T. *Prison on trial*, Sage, 1990

McAllister, D., Bottomley, K . & Liebling, A. F*rom custody to community: throughcare for young offenders*, Aldershot: Avebury, 1992

McDermott, K. "We have no problem: the experience of racism in prison", N*ew Community,* 16 (2), 1990; 213-28

Mitchell, B. "Preparing life sentence prisoners for release", *Howard Journal,* 31 (3), 1992; 224-39

National Association for the Care and Resettlement of Offenders, *Black communities and the probation service: working together,* Report of a sub-committee of the NACRO Race Issues Advisory Committee, NACRO, 1991

National Association for the Care and Resettlement of Offenders, *Race policies into action, the implementation of equal opportunities policies in criminal justice agencies,* Report of the NACRO Race Issues Advisory Committee, NACRO, 1992

National Association of Probation Officers, *Access to justice,* Proceedings of a professional conference, NAPO, 1987

National Association of Probation Officers, "Advice/information for women about to start prison secondments - some strategies for survival", Trade Union Organisation Committee paper TUO41/91, mimeo, NAPO, 1991

National Association of Probation Officers, *HIV/AIDS policy document,* NAPO, 1992

National Association of Probation Officers, "Work with men who abuse women and/or children - guidelines for branch negotiation", Probation Practice Committee paper , 22/90, mimeo, NAPO, 1990

Nellis, M. "Towards a new view of probation values", in (eds.) Hugman, R. & Smith, D. *Ethics and social work,* Routledge, forthcoming, 1995

Nellis, M. "What is to be done about probation training?", in (eds.) May, T. & Vass, T. *Working with offenders,* forthcoming, 1995a

Parsloe, P. *The work of the probation and after-care officer,* Routledge & Kegan Paul, 1967

Player, P. "Women's prisons after Woolf", in (eds.) Player, E. & Jenkins, M. *Prisons after Woolf: reform through riot,* Routledge, 1994

Preece, A. "Being gay in prison", *Probation Journal* ,40 (2), 1993; 85-7

Prison Service, *National framework for the throughcare of offenders in custody to the completion of supervision in the community*, Home Office, 1994

Raban, T. "Removed from the community: prisoners and the probation service", in (ed.) Harding, J. *Probation and the community*, Tavistock, 1987

Ralli, R. "Health care in prisons", in (eds.) Player, E. & Jenkins, M. *Prisons after Woolf: reform through riot*, Routledge, 1994

Raynor, P., Smith, D. & Vanstone, M. *Effective probation practice*, Macmillan, 1994

Roberts, J. "The relationship between the community and the prison", in (eds.) Player, E. & Jenkins, M. *Prisons after Woolf: reform through riot*, Routledge, 1994

Rojek, C., Peacock, G. & Collins, S. *Social work and received ideas*, Routledge, 1988

Ross, R. R. & Fabiano, E. A. *Time to think: a cognitive model of delinquency prevention and offender rehabilitation*, Johnson City: Academy of Arts and Sciences, 1985

Shaw, S. "Race issues: brickbats . . . and bouquets?", *Prison Report*, 22, Spring 1993

Sim, J. "Reforming the penal wasteland: a critical review of the Woolf Report", in Player, E. & Jenkins, M. (eds.), *Prisons after Woolf: reform through riot*, Routledge, 1994

South Yorkshire Probation Service, *Probation, race and anti-racism*, Sheffield, SYPS, 1993

Thomas, P. "HIV/AIDS in prisons", *Howard Journal* 29 (1) 1990 1-13

Thomas, P. & Costigan, R. "Health care or punishment? Prisoners with HIV/AIDS", *Howard Journal*, 31 (4), 1992; 321-6

Thomas, T. "Confidentiality: the loss of a concept?", *Practice*, 2 (4), 1988; 358-72

Tumim, S., Jenkins, D. & Boddis, S. "Crying Woolf: has the report impacted on life for prisoners?", *Criminal Behaviour and Mental Health*, 3, 1993; 484-90

Waite, I. "Too little, too bad", *Probation Journal*, 41 (2), 1994; 85, 92-4

Walker, H. & Beaumont, B. *Probation work: critical theory and socialist practice*, Oxford: Basil Blackwell, 1981

Warner, S. *Making amends: justice for victims and offenders*, Aldershot: Avebury, 1992

Williams, B. Bail information: an evaluation of the scheme at HM Prison Moorland, Bradford: Horton, 1992

Williams, B. "Caring professionals or street-level bureaucrats? The case of probation officers' work with prisoners", *Howard Journal* 31 (4) 1992; 263-75 (1992a)

Williams, B. "The transition from prison to community", in (eds.) May, T. & Vass, T. *Working with offenders* (provisional title), Sage, forthcoming 1995

Williams, B "Towards justice in probation work with prisoners", in (eds.) Ward, D. & Lacey, D. *Towards greater justice,* Whiting & Birch, 1994

Williams, B. "What is happening to prison education?", *Prison Writing*, 1 (2), 1993; 40-56

Williams, B. *Work with prisoners*, Birmingham: Venture, 1991

Worrall, A. *"Have you got a minute?" The changing role of prison boards of visitors*, Prison Reform Trust, 1994

SEVEN: ALCOHOL AND DRUG PROBLEMS: PROFESSIONAL CONTROVERSIES AND PROBATION CONTROL STRATEGIES.

Andrew Shephard

In a book concerned with discerning "principles" in different areas of probation work, both authors and readers are at the mercy of language which contains many potential meanings. To some, "principles" may be a way of encoding accumulated good practice into short statements which are easily translated for new recruits and outside agencies. ("We are in favour of the principle of voluntary treatment because all the evidence shows that compulsory treatment is less effective.") For others, "principles" may come to be articulated loudly at exactly that time when certainties are difficult to sustain, a rhetoric to disguise the turmoil within and a guide to correct thinking. ("We refuse to cooperate with compulsory treatment orders because they contradict the principle of equal access to medical services.") In other circumstances, "principles" serve to define the values of the speaker, explaining their chosen paradigm or worldview within which internal coherence is maintained. ("We are working on the principle that addiction is a behavioural problem, addicts are cognitive of the costs and benefits, and it is legitimate to increase the costs of the behaviour, via court orders, in order to encourage progress.")

The point about "principles" is that they are foundational, that they provide the accepted truths on which other actions are based. The search for fundamental truth was sustainable in a modernist, progressive world which, through the steady action of scientific enquiry into the nature of reality, promised a gradual revealing of social facts and progress towards a better society. The post-modernist challenge, which replaces the search for the truth with a celebration of many competing more-or-less effective truths, apparently takes the ground away from under those who seek universal principles. People who talk about "principles" in the 1990s can sound old-fashioned. Even politicians, for whom "principles" used to be the standard rhetoric, now more often employ a rhetoric of managerial pragmatism to explain problems and solutions.

We might go along with this, throw away all principles except cost effectiveness and managerial efficiency, and spend this chapter discussing different ways of managing people with alcohol and drug problems in the criminal justice system. Thankfully, the targets of our concern would almost certainly thwart our objectives: substance

137

misuse as a lifestyle is a state of anarchic non-participation in the respectable world and a symbolic attachment to a different sub-cultural network. Such networks are remarkably impervious to all the apparatus of state control systems, in which we can include the probation service.

One way to rescue "principles" from post-modern relativism is to do as I have done above, and view them **in action**. How are they used to convince? How are they used to argue the need for more resources? How are they used as weapons in a verbal war to attempt to settle disputes and controversies? (Lyotard 1984). I will briefly describe three main sources of principles used for arguing about alcohol and drug problems - scientific, sociological, and public health - and consider some of the controversies which they attempt to settle. In doing so, I will imagine that a probation team is reconsidering its approach to clients with alcohol and drug problems and trying to work out a strategy.

Throughout this century, controversy has surrounded the use of alcohol and drugs in Britain. Their potential to wreck individual lives and undermine the moral fibre and work ethic of whole communities has been much expressed and greatly exaggerated. Early this century, cocaine was discovered to be a serious threat to the morality of young women, and a small number of well-publicised drug scandals were used to gain acceptance of the first drug prohibition legislation (Kohn, 1992). The language of war has been used to describe the battle to prevent the extension of illegal drug markets. Punitive sentencing has been used to incarcerate "dealers" and organisers of the drug trade for very long periods. At the same time, some senior figures in some public agencies have admitted that the bad effects of drugs are much amplified by their illegality.

The controversy around alcohol has been equally fierce. At the beginning of the century, the Temperance Movement was extremely successful in persuading large numbers of people to sign the pledge of abstinence. The same movement, through the Church of England Temperance Society, was responsible for the first police court missionaries in 1876. Alcohol, and the desire to save people from its devastating effects, was there at the very conception of the Probation Service (King, 1958). Controversies about alcohol continue today. The latest, carried out with equal vehemence in academic journals and popular newspapers, argues that alcohol may have physical health benefits and re-examines the advisory limits of 21 units for men and 14 for women set by the Department of Health (Anderson *et al.* 1993).

Controversy surrounds not only the substances but also the people who use them. Are they a distinct group, especially susceptible to the addictive qualities of drugs? Are they victims of exploitative commercial or criminal networks? Are they people who have other problems, who use alcohol or drugs to escape a painful reality? A continuum of explanations exist, ranging from those which state that everyone is at risk if they drink or use drugs "too much", to those which argue that addicts are special people who can only be understood by other addicts.

These controversies are extensively investigated in books and journals, but, in common with much activity in the field of social science, the research and explanation have resulted in the formulation of very few sustainable social facts about alcohol and drug use. Even apparently simple questions such as whether someone with an alcohol problem can safely resume social drinking divides the alcohol field into different camps and many years of flag waving (Heather and Robertson, 1981). This could pose a problem for a probation team seeking to establish a strategy for responding to probationers who appear to have problems with alcohol and drugs. How can you devise a strategy if you cannot settle simple questions about the nature and size of the problem?

One reason for the confusion is that our knowledge of alcohol and drug problems is informed by three distinct paradigms, each of which has its own assumptions and each suggests its own responses. At one extreme are scientific explanations, which focus on the chemical properties of substances and the physical and psychological properties of humans. At the other extreme are sociological explanations, which see all drug use as social behaviour. A third position, which might be called the public health explanation, has become prominent in the past twenty years. This is essentially a compromise between the scientific and the sociological explanations, and uses epidemiological analysis to explain and to attempt to influence alcohol and drug use.

What does each of these approaches suggest in the way of principles and practice? What strategy should our probation team adopt, given the logic of a particular approach? I will look briefly at each approach and then, for those who hate to choose, I will propose a fourth way of describing alcohol and drug problems, using actor-network theory (Law, 1992) which provides a way of resolving the apparent contradictions between the other three approaches, and which suggests another framework for providing help via the active building of partnerships.

SCIENTIFIC EXPLANATIONS

One of the fascinating aspects of drugs and alcohol is that they provide one of the points of intersection between traditional science and social science. Unlike crime or poverty, we are talking here about identified substances which can be analysed, measured, quantified, tested on rats and humans in the laboratory. Once the drug is inside the human, however, the problems of behaviour measurement and analysis assert themselves. Undaunted, the scientific community continues to produce a deluge of papers with incredible titles, exploring ever more convoluted and minute aspects of drug and alcohol use. As more atoms of knowledge about addiction are discovered, its real nature will be revealed. Although such research is increasingly geared to incorporating social factors, the methodology is that of traditional science: comparative surveys, controlled experiments, variable analysis.

The assumption behind the scientific approach is that we live in world made up of causes and effects, and that there is a scientific reality to addiction which, when cultural differences are accounted for, is a universal experience brought about by the chemical properties of substances combined with the physical properties of humans. In other words, addiction is a state which can be measured, induced in the laboratory, even predicted given certain doses of the drug. Having understood the aetiology of addiction, treatments can be devised. These can then be tested on groups of addicts, in the hospital or in the field. Comparisons can be made between those receiving the treatment and those not receiving it. Although it is very difficult to control for all the possible variables, the result should be an indication that some treatments have more success than others.

Treatments are devised by (medical) professionals and traditionally take place in a hospital or clinic. Ironically, most treatments for drug problems involve the prescribing of different drugs. Three main types of prescribing can be identified: drugs to mask the unpleasant effects of withdrawal, usually tranquillisers; drugs which make the taking of the desired drug difficult because they precipitate a violent adverse reaction, usually disulfiram (antabuse) or naltrexone for opiates; and thirdly, drugs which have chemical similarities to the drug users' preferred substances and which create similar effects, such as methadone for opiate users or heminevrin for alcohol users. Some practitioners now advocate the next step in this logic of treatment, which means simply prescribing the drug in the form the user prefers. These drug treatments are, or rather should be, accompanied by talking treatments like counselling, the main purpose of which is to ensure that the patient stays in the treatment.

Success cannot be claimed unless the patient completes the treatment.

In practice, the whole range of treatments devised by psychiatric medicine have been thrown at alcoholics and drug addicts at some time or other, from psychotherapy to electric shock therapy. New treatments are greeted with enthusiasm, but disillusion soon sets in as the practical problems of delivering the treatment assert themselves. There are many reasons for this, the most obvious one being that medicine requires control of the patient: they must do what they are told by the expert. This is not generally the case with people who have drug and alcohol problems: people smuggle drugs and alcohol into the detoxification unit, fail to take their antabuse tablet, get stoned on tranquillisers, and sell their prescribed methadone to obtain other drugs.

Although group therapies have been embraced in many clinical settings, the focus of the scientific approach is on the individual. The unit of measurement for success or failure is the individual case record, and there is an assumption behind the identification of individual pathologies that cure is potentially possible, given the correct treatment and enough of it. If every individual with an alcohol or drug problem would consent to treatment and if there were sufficient resources, then the problems could be eventually cured. Sadly, far from gradually clearing up the problem of addiction through treatment, the numbers of people with identified alcohol and drug problems are increasing, and new forms of addiction and addictive behaviour are being discovered all the time.

If our probation team adopts the scientific approach, their strategy will be geared to providing access to clinical services. Detoxification will be a high priority, requiring good liaison with hospital consultants and community psychiatric nursing services. Scientific work is essentially professional and specialist work, so clients will be encouraged to participate in specialist services to receive drug and drug related treatments. Those who fail to take advantage of this offer will be described as "not motivated": but eventually, because addiction gets progressively worse, they will be driven into the arms of specialist helpers. Successes will be attributed to the effectiveness of the treatment programme, failure to the insufficient motivation of the participant.

SOCIOLOGICAL EXPLANATIONS

Sociologists would see no contradiction in the parallel extension of the clinical addiction specialisms and the continued discovery of more addictive behaviour in the population. Because addiction is socially defined behaviour, its boundaries can be drawn almost anywhere. A term which used to be reserved for signalling the immediate danger of death or at least severe psychological harm is now extended to smoking cigarettes and drinking coffee, exercise and shopping.

In contrast to the individualism of scientific explanations, socio-logical explanations identify social groups and sub-cultures. Curing individuals of their addiction is a hopeless task because addiction problems are only a symptom of deeper societal problems such as unemployment and deprivation. To talk of "cure" is a nonsense if individuals return from their treatment into the conditions which caused the dependence on drugs or alcohol in the first place.

Sociological insights, created through participant observation studies and qualitative surveys of drug users, paint a different picture of the world of the addict. (For an example of this entertaining literature, see Young (1971).) It is a colourful world, full of ritual and symbolic activity geared to identification with a subculture. These subcultures have their own routines, language, moral codes, and entry requirements. Drugs and alcohol are part of the language, the means of exchange, and a source of purposeful activity, but the actual effects of the drugs are relatively unimportant. Since people know what to expect from drugs, they tend to act in the expected way whether the drug is real or fake. Drugs are very plastic in their effects, interpreted differently by different groups at different times.

Removing an individual from this world is unlikely to have any effect because he or she will be replaced by another recruit. The extent of poverty and exclusion from the material benefits of society means that there is an endless potential supply of people to join drug subcultures or homeless drinkers on the streets. Society needs such groups of people, as a moral warning to those who fail to strive and work hard, as a pool of casual labour who can drop in and out of the labour market as demand requires, and to provide useful employment for the middle class helping professions. The labelling of out-groups like alcoholics is part of the process by which mainstream society reassures itself and justifies its own obsessions like driving cars. (Can you think of a habit which kills about 4,000 people each year in the UK, wrecks the lives of tens of thousands more, costs thousands of pounds per year to maintain, raises blood pressure, pollutes innocent bystanders etc?).

What kind of approaches to dealing with drug and alcohol problems do sociological explanations suggest? After all, sociology is not much use if it is only descriptive: the mission of sociology was to provide an accumulation of social facts which would inform policy makers and enable social progress. By and large, it has not succeeded in establishing a body of social facts which can be defended: no universal laws of societal development have been found to parallel the laws of natural science. Sociological knowledge has limitations in providing solutions to specific problems.

If our probation team is following sociological explanations of drug and alcohol problems, what kind of strategies should they employ? The answer would be to engage in a variety of political and social action aimed at reducing poverty and unemployment, raising the political consciousness of the underclass so that they would reject the labels of powerlessness placed upon them by the Establishment. There are obvious contradictions in a state agency like the probation service undertaking such a programme of action. Given the resources of the service, the size of the problem of deprivation, not to mention the wider political climate, such an approach fails to sound believable. Recognising this, our probation team might scale down its objectives to more-manageable tasks such as mitigating the bad effects of deprivation through support and advocacy. By forming a coalition with other sources of help in the statutory and voluntary sectors, campaigning on issues like homelessness may serve to create the political action that ameliorates the situation for the most deprived.

PUBLIC HEALTH EXPLANATIONS

Public health explanations borrow from both scientific and socio-logical perspectives. Alcohol and drug use is seen as occurring in populations. Different levels of use are determined, and statistics are compiled which show, for example, that 14 per cent of men drink over thirty-five units of alcohol per week. (Alcohol Concern, 1987). Since high levels of drinking are associated with a number of diseases and increased risk of accidents, campaigns are launched both at specific types of drinking behaviour (for example, drinking and driving advertising campaigns) and at generally reducing the numbers drinking at over the given level. The Department of Health in the UK has issued specific targets for the reduction of numbers of men and women drinking over recommended "sensible" limits (21 units for men and 14 for women) by the year 2005.

Public health explanations have gained a lot of ground in the past twenty years, with the development of national campaigns and local health promotion units inside the National Health Service. The approach appears to be value free and non-judgemental: everyone must be in favour of improved health, and it is an implicit assumption that improved health and a longer life are synonymous with increased happiness and well-being. The public is presented as a unified mass, sharing the same goal of better health.

Despite the apparent rationality of the public health approach, there are flaws which have to be mentioned. Firstly, how are "safe" limits of drug use arrived at? The contradictory evidence concerning the possible protective effects of alcohol in relation to heart disease (Anderson *et al.*, 1993) demonstrate the difficulties. There are many problems in conducting studies which try to match behaviour with health. Will people tell the truth about their substance use? Do they really know how much of a substance they usually have? How long do you have to be above the "safe" limits before health is affected? A month, a year, a decade, or half a century? The complexities of controlling for other variables such as smoking or lack of exercise, poor housing or traffic pollution, further muddy the waters.

It would not be hard to come to the conclusion that public health advice about drugs and alcohol is cultural statements dressed up in statistical language. When the general population is analysed in terms of classes or areas of relative deprivation, health mortality is seen to be concentrated in areas where poverty is greatest. The idealised middle class lifestyle of public health campaigns (low fat, safe sex, regular exercise, the occasional glass of wine), is contrasted with chips, promiscuity, couch potato, drunk-every-Friday-night, working class lifestyle. The former lifestyle will save the country millions through lower absenteeism and fewer demands on the health service, and it is the duty of all good citizens to persuade the working classes to change their preferences.

Because the public health perspective looks at large populations and statistical likelihoods, it catches many more people in its net. It enrols not just those who medically speaking seem to be ill as a result of their substance use, but also millions more who appear to be behaving the same (drinking over so many units, for example) as those who are actually ill. Who is to be helped? The 1 or 2 per cent who appear to have real and current problems, or the 14 per cent who must have problems because they are drinking "too much" at the moment? The public health perspective says that resources are much better spent if directed at the whole of the problem group, because that way prevention of more serious harm can be achieved. The 1 or 2 per cent who actually have problems are very hard to help and probably too far gone to save from their fate.

The claim for effective prevention of harm is based on a belief in the effectiveness of large scale social engineering. It suggests that the drug using habits of a population can be manipulated by campaigns, laws, and public policies. In practice, public health campaigns are almost impossible to evaluate because so many factors influence the drug use of populations. Drug use is fundamentally social behaviour, and people tend to copy the behaviour of those around them. Trends in a population's use of drugs tend to be closely linked with other social changes, for example, women using cocaine in the era of emancipation around the first world war (Kohn, 1992). The continued use of prohibited drugs by upwards of 1.5 million people in Britain (ISDD, 1993) illustrates the limits of social engineering in controlling behaviours.

If our probation team accepts the logic of the public health explanation of alcohol and drug problems, then the strategy will be broad based and aimed at probation clients generally. Surveys of caseloads will have already demonstrated that a high proportion of clients abuse drink and drugs. The team might participate in national events such as "Drinkwise Day" and "European Drug Prevention Week". They will have adequate supplies of leaflets about safe drinking and drug use. They will run educational groups which will give clients the facts so that they can make their own rational, balanced decisions. Our probation team will join the growing army of middle class professionals who know how to live a good and healthy life and have a mission to make other people live like they do.

A FOURTH PERSPECTIVE: ACTOR-NETWORKS

Are we any closer to understanding what substance misuse problems are, or how they should be responded to? Scientific methods say we should discover effective treatments and apply them to individual pathologies. Sociologists say that society produces sickness in people and we should change social structures to reduce deprivation. Public health professionals claim that attitudes and behaviours can be engineered to produce healthier people. A similar scenario appears with other social problems, like road accidents, for example. One perspective blames bad drivers (individual pathology), another the lack of public transport (social structure), and the third says that if only we had lower speed limits and better road signs, accidents would be reduced (traffic engineering).

These different explanations of a road accident are competing descriptions of reality which try to convince us that they deserve the resources to tackle the problem. With drug and alcohol problems, it is not that one explanation has discovered the nature, cause, and solution whilst the others have failed to do so, but that each explanation is competing to convince those with resources that their interpretation is the correct one. A war is waged with books, research reports, graphs, statistics, and case examples. Because so few facts about addiction are accepted for very long, the controversy and the competition for resources are likely to continue.

Systems theory, familiar to many readers, was borrowed, like many concepts in social science, from observations of the natural world of ecology. Essentially interactionist in perspective, systems theory stressed the interconnectedness of human relationships, the collaborative support inherent in such systems, and the tendency of ecological systems to move back towards equilibrium when balance has been disturbed. A more recent borrowing from the study of science, actor-network theory (Latour, 1987), provides some startling insights into the way networks have been built out of the raw materials of documents, devices, and disciplined people (Law, 1992). Such networks, for example telecommunications systems, multi-national manufacturers, satellite television companies, have grown extremely robust and extensive in the modern era, transcending national boundaries and transforming concepts of organisation. In practice, day-to-day life involves, for we human actors, passage from the ambit of one network to another: transport networks, employment networks, television networks, leisure networks. Each network has its own architecture, devices (technologies), conditions of entry and departure, and they all have the ability to evoke suitable behaviour. Such networks are effective because they are able to combine people (who know how they should behave), technologies, and operating instructions in a way that allows predictable results.

We can now consider our probation team as being part of a network of state agencies, charged one way or another, with producing and implementing a wide and changing variety of control strategies to manage, alter, suppress, or extinguish behaviours which are problematic to the modern state. The probation network, like others, is constructed with heterogeneous materials, including buildings, computers, documents, and filing cabinets, all of which are contributors to probation activities.

One target of probation activities is people with drug and alcohol problems. Their behaviours attract attention because of they often ignore signs and symbols, produce behaviours in the wrong place, and fail to participate reliably (as disciplined people) in formal networks.

If we shift the focus slightly from the probation team to the probation clients with drug and alcohol problems, they can be seen as potential members of two different networks. One network (the informal network) made up of drugs, alcohol, supply networks,

146

means of obtaining money, drug routines, places to hang out, and the probation team: the other (the control network) made up of the detoxification ward, the residential programme, the appointment with the community team counsellor, the harm-reduction group at the day centre, the activities project, and the probation team. It is likely that, at any one time, far more probation clients are in the first network than in the second. Many others move backwards and forwards between the two networks, depending on their current situation: an impending court appearance, for example, may lead to some short term compliance with the control network. Free movement from one network to another is not entirely possible. There are costs associated with leaving the informal network (other network members will feel let down and may apply pressure to remain) and with leaving the control network: sanctions may be applied through breach proceedings, future access may be denied or made more difficult.

Both networks have an imperfect ability to evoke correct behaviour and command allegiance. The role of our probation team has become both easier and more difficult. Easier, because it no longer has to bother about the competing claims of medical treatments, public health initiatives, or structural cures. They are just a competition between other networks trying to persuade resource providers to back their schemes. More difficult, because the task is not to temporarily detach the client from their informal network and place them for two hours in an alcohol education group, but to provide a more permanent alternative which has the coherence to hold them in place for a longer time.

This is a quite different way of viewing "treatment" in all its various guises. Treatment interventions, in the language and methodology of science, have made implicit assumptions about a world of cause and effect. We start with a problem (drug addiction). We devise a treatment (methadone prescribing). We can measure the effect, the outcome, of that treatment. The treatment will cause change, and we can, by observing and counting results over a period of time, predict what that change will be. In practice, after several years of methadone prescribing, we are left with yet more uncertainty. We do not know if methadone prescribing reduces harm by providing an easy access to drugs, or increases harm by extending the lifespan of addictive behaviour. Since most addictive behaviours are self-limiting and not influenced significantly by professional help (Orford, 1985), perhaps many of those 1980s opiate users would have given up long ago but for regular supplies of methadone. (It must be acknowledged that that logic of methadone prescribing was much more influenced by the threat of the spread of HIV infection amongst injecting drug users than by a belief that it would help to cure addiction (ACMD, 1993).)

The message in this is that behaviours are specific to situations, that they are evoked by network participation. People moving from one network to another adopt the behaviours they see in the people around them. Most behaviour is simply copied. It is fanciful to imagine that someone who attends a group on drugs will continue non-drug-using behaviour once outside of that group network - unless it is possible to build an extended network, open to our probation client, where non-using behaviour is the normal behaviour. Treatments of various kinds can be very effective whilst the treatment continues. But measured outcomes for drug and alcohol treatments are poor once the treatment has finished, unless the treatment has provided access to another, non-drug-using, network.

I have talked about the drug-and alcohol-using network as a single idea for the sake of convenience. Although many probation clients use several different substances problematically, there are important differences in the construction of the networks. The prohibited-drug network is rather different from the alcohol network, the illegality of drugs ensuring that the drug network is informal, mostly invisible, untaxable and uncontrollable. An industry worth hundreds of millions of pounds per year is run without business plans, annual reports, marketing departments, or advertising campaigns. The alcohol network, in contrast, is bound solidly and openly into the cultural and economic life of the country and it is able to mount effective lobbies of government when its interests are attacked.

DEFINING A STRATEGY

How is the probation team, a modest player in the criminal justice network, able to influence the alcohol network or the drug network? In defining a strategy, the probation team has to take account of the effectiveness of drug and alcohol networks, acknowledge the constraints of the probation and criminal justice network, and consider the opportunities for co-opting other helping agency networks to achieve probation goals (historically, the favoured technique of the probation idea).

THE EFFECTIVENESS OF DRUG AND ALCOHOL NETWORKS.

The strategy must take account of the observation that people are tied firmly into drug-and alcohol-using networks, that for most of the time this is unproblematic, and that even when alcohol or drug use is having some negative consequences for the individual, the ability of the networks to create powerful attachments is usually dominant.

The implications of this for strategy are:

a)   most clients will appear "unmotivated" to leave their current networks and this may as well be accepted;

b)   persuasion to try an alternative network (some kind of treatment) will be most effective when the client is already looking for another network to join - perhaps because of difficulties (threats, unpaid debts) in their existing network;

c)   people do not have fixed preferences and appear ambivalent, producing different language and behaviour according to which network they currently inhabit (remember the ability of actor-networks to evoke the required behaviours from human actors): it is no surprise if people appear to change their minds, many times, about drug or alcohol use, as they move from one network to another. This should be accepted, and not taken as an indication of failure or success.

CONSTRAINTS IMPOSED BY THE PROBATION AND CRIMINAL JUSTICE NETWORKS

Our probation team is limited by certain rules and expectations, one of which is that it will only work with identified offenders for specific purposes and specific periods of time. The requirement to focus on local and national objectives, to record and measure outputs, to implement national standards in carrying out probation orders, has the effect of reducing the likelihood of being able to plan a campaign which engaged with a defined local drug problem. Most of the target group of such a campaign would be technically outside of the brief of the modern, targeted, probation team.

The Criminal Justice Act (1991) represented a further attempt to target specific sentences, with requirements for drug and alcohol treatments of various kinds, at high tariff offenders. Most drug and alcohol offenders commit large numbers of relatively minor crimes, and do not technically qualify for the high tariff "treatment" options. Furthermore, drugs remains such an emotive issue that courts continue to send high tariff drug offenders (trade organisers) straight to jail.   Another dilemma lies in the fact that people with drug and alcohol problems are in practice least likely to match up to the reporting requirements of the modern probation order, let alone a more complex community sentence made up of a package of attendances at various groups and activities. The effect of decreased officer discretion in the operation of probation and other formal orders cannot yet be assessed, but the legions of offenders with drug and alcohol problems who would require specific probation packages to tackle their problems have not appeared. Use of residential treatment has not increased, and the numbers sent from courts remain just a few hundred per year. A piece of research in London suggested that only 20 per cent of those completed even a short assessment period (Boother,1991).

It is interesting to note that, nearly a century ago, an "Inebriates Act" provided for detention for up to three years in an inebriate reformatory. These were establishments run, like today's care homes and rehabilitation units, by voluntary bodies or local authorities. The detention was provided in addition to any punishment for the offence committed. Despite huge public concern about drunkenness and the apparent relationship between alcohol consumption and petty crime, only a few hundred were sent to the inebriate reformatories each year, about the same number who go from courts to residential treatment today. This was very much fewer than was expected. A departmental committee, reporting on the effect of the new law in 1908, called for powers to send people to the reformatories irrespective of whether or not they had committed an offence. Parliament did not find time to pass such legislation (Garland, 1985). There always seems to have been a problem in matching the assumed relationship between alcohol, drugs, and crime with actual people who fit the criteria.

In essence, the problem for our probation team is that the probation service, and the rest of the criminal justice system, takes a view of criminal behaviour which suggests that it is somehow <u>inside</u> the individual. It seeks to punish, persuade, or reform individual offenders when they represent a small fraction, at any one time, of the people with those behaviours. This could never represent a feasible method of dealing with social problems such as crime or alcohol and drug misuse (Harris,1992).

CO-OPTING OTHER NETWORKS TO ACHIEVE PROBATION OBJECTIVES.

Our probation team may decide to offer clients direct help in dealing with their drug and alcohol problems. They may provide leaflets, have posters on harm reduction in the waiting room, run groups for those whose offences are in some way related to their substance use. These will use a range of techniques, depending on the skills and interests of the group facilitators. There is no conclusive evidence to suggest that one kind of group is more effective than another (Brown and Caddick, 1993), but alcohol education groups which have a behavioural element (drinking diaries, homework) above and beyond information-giving achieve a higher retention rate (Baldwin, 1990).

Whatever direct services the probation team is able to provide, they are only likely to have an effect whilst the drug or alcohol misuser is a member of the group. Our strategy will therefore have to rely principally on the ability of the team to form formal and informal partnerships with other organisations, the goal being to provide an alternative network for the drug or alcohol user to join.

The scale and form of such partnerships will depend on local conditions, but certain principles will encourage good partnerships and relevant networks. Good communication is essential, and this can be achieved through membership of voluntary agency committees and through secondments to community drug and alcohol teams. Partnerships should be varied, so that the probation client has access to different services with different emphases: harm-reduction and controlled-use strategies should be allowed for, but those who want to try abstinence from the substance should be brought together to provide peer support.

Services should be easily accessible, and this means a concentration on informal networks which do not impose long waiting lists or complex admission procedures. Informal networks should allow for the proliferation of small groups and organisations, meeting the requirements of different people - women with children, family members, ethnic groups with different drinking and drug-using norms and behaviours. The aim of such informal networks is to allow people to cross over the barrier from "person with problem" and become a "person who can help others". Specialist facilities with a clinical orientation cannot easily provide the means for the client to cross that barrier. Community-based services, such as community businesses, training workshops, supported self-help networks, all have the potential to maximise involvement, member-ship, and participation. In some areas, people who have used drug and alcohol services have been helped to form service user groups and now have a role in the formal planning systems of joint planning. One voluntary agency is encouraging clients to set up their own emergency telephone help system for people experiencing relapse problems. A network which can provide day care, training opportunities, friends, meaningful activity, someone to talk to if difficulties occur, self-help initiatives, and access to other, more robust, networks like college courses and employment, is one which provides probation clients with some opportunity to change direction.

The existence of such networks is fragile and dependent on the operation of community care legislation, local authority funding, and the operation of the quasi-market of care which is currently developing. Hopefully, our probation team will decide to be a player in that market, and will have partnership resources delegated to it to enable access to clients who want to move away from the problems of drugs and alcohol.

References

Advisory Council on the Misuse of Drugs. *Aids and Drug Misuse Update.* HMSO, 1993

Alcohol Concern. *The Drinking Revolution: building a campaign for safer drinking.* Alcohol Concern, 1987

Anderson, P. *et al.* The risk of alcohol. *Addiction*, Vol 88, 11, 1993; 1493-1508

Baldwin, S. (ed) *Alcohol Education and Offenders.* Batsford, 1990

Boother, M. Drug misusers: Rethinking Residential Rehabilitation. *Probation Journal*, Vol. 38, 4, 1991; 181-185

Brown, A. & Caddick, B. (eds) *Groupwork with Offenders.* Whiting & Birch 1993

Garland, D. *Punishment and Welfare.* Aldershot, Gower, 1985

Harris, R. *Crime, Criminal Justice, and the Probation Service.* Routledge, 1992

Heather, N. & Robertson, I. *Controlled Drinking.* Methuen, 1981

Institute for the Study of Drug Dependence. *National Audit of Drug Misuse in Britain 1992.* ISDD, 1993

King, J. (ed). *The Probation Service*, Butterworth, 1958

Kohn, M. Dope Girls. *The Birth of the British Drug Underground.* Lawrence and Wishart , 1992

Latour, B. *Science in Action*. Harvard University Press, 1987 .

Law, J. "Notes on the theory of the actor-network: ordering, strategy and heterogeneity". *Systems Practice*, 5, 1992; 379-93.

Lyotard, J-F. *The Postmodern Condition: A Report on Knowledge.* Manchester University Press, 1984

Orford, J. *Excessive Appetites: A Psychological view of Addictions.* Wiley, 1985

Young, J. The role of the police as Amplifiers of Deviancy, Negotiators of Reality and Translators of Fantasy in *Images of Deviance*, Cohen, S. (ed.) Harmondsworth: Penguin, 1971 .

EIGHT: HIV, AIDS AND PROBATION PRACTICE

Una Padel

The arrival of the HIV epidemic in Britain has had far-reaching implications for the work of health and welfare services. These have extended far beyond work with individuals directly, or even indirectly, affected by HIV. As the very nature of confidentiality has been minutely re-evaluated, new ethical dilemmas have arisen, and health education strategies have changed.

The first AIDS publicity campaign, featuring tombstones and icebergs, set out to frighten. The inextricable links between HIV, sex and drug use enabled the press to capitalise on the fear engendered with an avalanche of sensational stories. The result was that the level of public awareness of AIDS was very high by the mid-1980s. Unfortunately this was not generally matched by levels of knowledge about HIV transmission routes or the behavioural modifications necessary to avoid infection. The higher prevalence of AIDS in some African countries and the early identification of HIV among gay men led to an apparent increase in racism and homophobia, or perhaps simply enabled attitudes which could no longer be voiced to resurface with a new "respectability". The fact that HIV transmission is usually associated with sex or injecting drug use led to a high degree of blame being attached to those with the virus. This was echoed in the phrase "high risk groups" used to describe gay men, prostitutes and injecting drug users by many agencies (including some probation services) in the latter part of the 1980s. This inaccurate and unhelpful terminology describes people by their lifestyle rather than by HIV risk. It offered the opportunity for stereotypes to be confirmed and took no account of the changes individuals made to reduce their risk levels (for example the use of sterile injecting equipment or safe sex) leaving those outside the "high risk groups" to indulge in risky activities with a false sense of security.

Probation services have been relatively slow to develop HIV policies and, even when they did, initial attempts were sometimes unclear or based on inaccurate information. As recently as 1989 officers in one service were being advised to interview clients known or suspected of having HIV near an open window. At the same time, in a neighbouring area, staff were advised to avoid being scratched by cats, presumably on the basis that the animals' claws may still be bloodied from previous victims!

Since 1989 an increasing number of services have adopted training strategies and developed guidance for staff. The Association of Chief Officers of Probation (ACOP) produced a useful document entitled "HIV, AIDS, Confidentiality and the Probation Service" in 1989 and many services have used it as a basis for their own local guidance documents. The National Association of Probation Officers (NAPO) produced an HIV/AIDS policy in 1992 and in the same year CCETSW published a guide to required levels of competence in relation to HIV and AIDS for social work students. These documents provide a framework within which the complex issues relating to HIV and probation practice may be considered.

HIV ISSUES AND PROBATION PRACTICE

HIV highlights the ethical bases upon which social work in general operates, it raises unique problems in relation to the criminal justice system and the relationship of the probation service to other agencies, and it brings into question the role of probation staff as potential providers of specialist information and health education to groups of people who may otherwise be hard to reach.

For many years social work training has adopted non-judgementalism as a basic imperative. Respect for the individual and the right to self-determination have been central to the development of good practice. As awareness of the effects of oppression and the many forms it takes has increased, social work professionals have been encouraged to tackle racism, sexism and heterosexism and to evaluate practice to seek out and correct any unconscious prejudice. Press coverage of HIV brought to the fore many of the negative stereotypes upon which prejudice is based. The main function of this was to convince white heterosexuals that they were safe from HIV and need not modify their lifestyles.

The notion that people with HIV were somehow to blame for the situation has been particularly difficult to deal with. HIV-awareness education has not necessarily helped either. An important element of most basic HIV education is information about the very specific transmission routes of the virus, and about its fragility and inability to survive outside the body. It is of course important to highlight transmission routes so that people are able to keep themselves safe and not panic about non-existent risks. Unfortunately the unintended by-product of this information is often to reinforce the attitude that if HIV is not easily communicable, then those who have the virus must have been excessively careless to contract it. Thus pre-existing prejudices about irresponsibility, promiscuity and hedonism are confirmed. It is very important that issues such as power differences in sexual situations, peer pressure, cultural norms in drug taking situations and the influence of alcohol and drugs on behaviour are properly emphasised in HIV education if the potential for blame is not to be increased.

CONFIDENTIALITY

Confidentiality is fundamental to social work practice, but HIV has forced a minute re-examination of the way information is collected, shared and stored. As the HIV panic hit Britain, staff in social welfare and health agencies felt they needed to keep themselves safe. The most obvious method seemed to be to identify those with the virus and take special precautions in relation to them. Those most worried were often members of staff who would be unlikely to be aware of confidential information, the clerical and cleaning staff. Defenders of the need for confidentiality were often in the more powerful position of knowing, or having access to, information about individuals and to the training necessary to be more confident about routes of transmission so that they were able to feel safe.

Sales of polystyrene cups must have increased dramatically during this period as a general unease about the information that HIV was not transmissible through saliva seemed to pervade the "caring" agencies. At the same time probation and health centre waiting areas were adorned with patronising posters urging everyone to hug people with AIDS.

A prurient interest has been shown by the press in the activities of people known to have HIV (particularly if they involve sex, drugs or violence) and the practice of isolating those known to have HIV in prisons was abandoned relatively recently. The potential for information contained in Social Enquiry Reports or Pre Sentence Reports to be leaked to the press at court, or to fall into the wrong hands at the prison reception area, resulted in a heightened awareness of the need to include only strictly relevant information in such reports. Probation officers devised alternative methods of passing information to sentencers, often via notes or doctors' letters handed in separately. If the defendant feels that the sentencers should be aware of his/her HIV status because of the likelihood of ill health or because it was a significant factor in the offence, then this seems to be the safest way of doing so whilst preserving the client's confidentiality. Although this may be the most practical way of ensuring that information remains confidential, steps should be taken to ensure that PSRs, which contain other personal information, do

157

not fall into the wrong hands.

Within the probation service confidentiality has usually been understood to mean that information is accessible to anyone within the service with a legitimate interest. The fact that information given to a particular officer by a client is likely to be recorded in the file (by a clerical worker), discussed with a senior probation officer during supervision, and to be accessible to the officer's colleagues, should the client call at a time when the officer is unavailable, is not always explained adequately to probation service clients. Sensitive information about relationships, sexuality, and health among other issues has always been included in probation records, but other than the "open records" debate there had been relatively little discussion about the routine recording of sensitive information. Because of the strongly emotive issues associated with HIV and the stigma attached there has been some controversy over the recording of this information. This debate is probably long overdue. The ACOP document "HIV, AIDS, Confidentiality and the Probation Service" cites as general principles:

- that confidentiality should be preserved in relation to HIV as much as with other information unless it can specifically be shown to be inappropriate

- that clients should not be disadvantaged in relation to confidentiality and HIV because of their involvement with the Probation Service

- that at the outset of contact with clients an explanation should be given of how confidentiality works in practice (i.e. access to information by others working in the probation service) so that they make an informed choice about sharing a confidence

- that where a confidence is to be shared a clear explanation should be given as to who will then have access to the information

- that probation staff should relate to everyone as if they are HIV positive so that safety does not depend on knowing an individual's HIV status

- that any member of staff facing a dilemma relating to HIV should be offered time for thinking by their line manager

The document examines the confidentiality issues likely to arise in relation to every aspect of probation work. It concludes that when work is undertaken with someone who is HIV positive, HIV status should be recorded in a similar way to any other information. This is for three reasons:

"i) if HIV status is not recorded, much of the work being undertaken will not be seen to make sense

ii) professional and public accountability cannot countenance selective recording of work undertaken

iii) to omit HIV from the record feeds into the mystification of HIV. It is hoped that, over time, sensitivity will gradually lessen. Implicit in this view is that clerical staff are within the boundary of confidentiality. It is therefore vital that they receive the necessary HIV training and it will also be essential to stress the fundamental requirement that they respect confidentiality in this area. This will go so far as to stress that, as with other probation staff, breaking of a confidence without permission will be seen as gross misconduct likely to lead to dismissal".

It goes on to suggest that staff should be discouraged from asking clients about their antibody status as the client may feel compelled to answer the question and the information would then have to be recorded.

The National Association of Probation Officers (NAPO) takes a different view on recording. In its HIV/AIDS Policy (1992) it asserts: "In the light of treating all contacts as being potentially HIV positive it becomes unnecessary and unprofessional to record HIV status. All of our recording is subjective and most members are aware of information about clients which is not recorded."

The ACOP suggestion that it might be better not to ask, so that the need to record such sensitive information does not arise, seems rather strange. Of course it would be inappropriate and impertinent for probation officers to routinely ask every client whether they have HIV. The power differential in a probation officer/client relationship is important and it is quite possible that a client may feel unable to refuse to answer such a question. Rather than asking a direct question it might be preferable to discuss HIV with clients in such a way that anyone wishing to work on HIV issues would be aware of the parameters of confidentiality, and of the access to information and assistance that disclosure might create. If a client does wish to discuss the fact that they have, or are concerned about HIV then it seems inappropriate to have a blanket policy about recording or not recording the information. Should the client disclose that they have HIV but does not wish to discuss it with the probation officer (for whatever reason), then there seems little value in recording the information. If one of the main areas of work concerns HIV then it is difficult to see how a decision not to record could be justified (unless the client specifically requests it).

Some of the most difficult situations likely to face probation staff occur when a client known to have HIV is putting someone else at risk without telling them. An example might be a client with HIV who has unprotected sex with a partner who is unaware of the situation. It is easy to assume that everyone should take responsibility for their own safety, but in many situations that assumption takes no account of the complexities of human relationships where the immediate need not to upset or offend the partner may take greater priority than avoiding an unknown risk. In the case of a long-term relationship it may be that the partner would regard themselves as being in a safe and monogamous situation. In fact the guidance on dealing with such situations is unequivocal. The probation officer cannot breach the confidence without the express permission of the client. The ACOP paper cites a General Medical Council statement issued in May 1988 which upheld a strict line on confidentiality but acknowledged that medical practitioners may decide to disclose where there is a "serious and identifiable risk to a specific individual". It suggests that probation staff should do all they can to persuade the client in this situation that the partner needs to be told, to the extent of offering to be present when the information is shared and helping to arrange support thereafter. The general principle developed earlier in the ACOP document that clients should not be disadvantaged in relation to confidentiality because of involvement with the Probation Service is useful in considering difficult situations of this sort.

HARM REDUCTION

The greatest impact of HIV on probation practice has involved work with drug users. It has reflected (and in most cases followed some way behind) a monumental change in the attitude of specialist drug agencies. The arrival of HIV in this country coincided with the new epidemic of heroin use in the early 1980s and this led to a major reassessment of priorities in the treatment of drug use. For almost twenty years there had been a widespread acceptance of abstinence as the only acceptable goal of drug treatment, and it was certainly central to the work of most probation officers with drug users (Bild and Hayes, 1990). In 1987 the Advisory Council on the Misuse of Drugs, in its report "AIDS and Drug Misuse, Part 1", suggested that HIV represented a greater threat to public health than drug misuse and that a wider range of services be offered to drug users on terms that were likely to be acceptable to them. They recommended that the range of services should include substitute prescribing and needle exchanges where drug users could obtain clean injecting equipment. This approach quickly became known as "harm reduction". The idea that opiate users could be prescribed methadone on a long term, maintenance, basis rather than as part of a detoxification contract was difficult for many to come to terms with. The preference shown by some drug users for injectible rather than orally administered methadone also created difficulties. Because decisions about an individual's maintenance or reduction, and about the prescription of injectible or oral methadone are taken by doctors rather than probation staff this situation may have forced the reassessment of the focus of work for some probation staff, but will not have created ethical dilemmas for individual probation officers. The idea of enabling those who continue to use illegal drugs to reduce the risks they face has been more problematic. As Bild and Hayes (1990) point out:

"Probation officers are in contact with people who experience their relationship with drugs as a positive, who are not seeking help and who would not present themselves to other agencies. Amongst this group will be a proportion who will become dependent and whose offending is likely to escalate. Of those who will be transitory, are some whose experimentation with drugs may include intravenous use or other unsafe practices: they all constitute a potential risk to themselves and others. They are in contact only because they have offended - and been caught!"

Of course the experience of being caught and convicted is likely to propel some drug users into treatment, or at least to encourage them to examine their drug use and the difficulties it is beginning to cause them. Others may not wish to engage with drug agencies for a variety of reasons, and for them the probation officer may be the only potential source of information about harm reduction. There is an inevitable paradox in the idea that someone sentenced to a probation order for possession of heroin may then receive information from that probation officer about how to use illegal drugs more safely.

It is entirely understandable that many probation officers have found the abandonment of abstinence-based work difficult. The probation service has its roots in the abstinence movement of the mid-nineteenth century and that tradition continues to some extent. Further discussion of the impact of the abstinence tradition on current probation practice is to be found in Andrew Shepard's chapter "Alcohol and drug problems: professional controversies and probation control strategies".

Harm reduction with those continuing to use illegal drugs also creates difficult ethical dilemmas. It often involves not only an acceptance of the fact that illegal personal drug use is continuing, but also that the fund-raising activities necessary to support the drug use (be they supplying drugs to others, shoplifting, burglary, etc) are continuing as well.

Of course the notion of harm reduction is not new to the probation service. Many probation officers have been informally and autonomously adopting harm-reduction strategies in relation to drug use and other crime for many years. In 1990 Inner London, Northumbria and Merseyside probation services were among the first to develop harm-reduction policies which were adopted by their respective probation committees. The Advisory Council on the Misuse of Drugs recommended in 1991 that "agencies working with drug misusing offenders should adopt the principles of harm reduction so as to avoid setting unrealistic goals".

In a policy statement issued in February 1993 the Inner London Probation Service responded to this by saying:

"ILPS accepts the recommendation of the Advisory Council on the Misuse of Drugs, that an additional aim of probation supervision, is to encourage the disclosure of drug misuse and to reduce the risk of harm to the offender and society, with particular reference to the spread of HIV/AIDS." (ILPS Policy Statement Drug and Alcohol Misusing Offenders, February 1993.)

The accompanying strategy document adds:

"This 'harm reduction' model and practice allows for a gradual and client determined progress towards the cessation of drug and alcohol misuse and any consequent criminal activity, rather than requiring misusers to stop using all drugs and alcohol immediately and regarding any relapse as failure. Abstinence may be appropriate for many offenders but not, in the first instance, for everyone." (ILPS Drug and Alcohol Misusers Strategy for Action with Offenders and Alleged Offenders, October, 1993.)

It is inevitably difficult to develop practice guidance which is precise enough to be helpful and yet flexible enough to assist probation staff with the dilemmas harm reduction creates. Guidance offered in the Northumbria Probation Service Dependency Manual suggests that officers should begin by setting clear ground rules for their contact with clients, in writing if necessary. Examples offered include:

"a) The probation officer accepts that the client is using illicit drugs and is willing to work on the problems this produces in confidence.

b) However any blatant evidence that the client is supplying drugs to others will lead to the police being notified.

c) Similarly, any concrete evidence of offending to buy drugs (i.e. evidence which could lead to a successful prosecution, stolen credit cards etc.) will also lead to police involvement." (Northumbria Probation Service Dependency Manual, Gardiner & Talbot, 1990.)

The guidelines emphasise the need for flexibility and offer the general principle that staff must

"act responsibly and be able to demonstrate that they have done so to the satisfaction of management, and other parties, if called upon to do so". (Gardiner & Talbot , 1990.)

This guidance is necessarily vague, but sets the parameters and legitimises a realistically high degree of awareness of illegal activity, as long as it falls short of the sort of evidence necessary to secure a conviction.

The adoption of harm reduction policies by probation services is a welcome development, but it falls short of guaranteeing drug users access to harm-reduction information. Some individual probation officers continue to hold strongly to the view that abstinence is the only legitimate goal of probation work with drug users. It is quite possible for officers with diametrically different views to be working alongside one another, creating an unacceptable inconsistency of approach. A client assigned to an individual officer (rather than a group work programme) is likely to have to work with the officer allocated. It is difficult for clients of the probation service to influence allocation or request a transfer. While the harm-reduction policies produced enable officers who so choose to work in this way, there is no compulsion upon them to do so. There is also no opportunity for clients to choose an officer likely to encourage them to reduce their risks while continuing to use drugs, as opposed to one with a conscientious objection to it. Although the very existence of harm-reduction policies seemed a major advance at first, it is now clear that development is needed. To ensure consistency there needs to be more than "encouragement" for officers to offer a harm reduction approach. Specific training about the rationale and practice of harm-reduction in a probation context must be provided if policies are to be fully implemented. Those who are unable to work in this way should be asked to discuss the situation with their line managers so that a strategy can be developed. This may involve referral of certain clients to other team members or greater co-operation with another agency. This issue was highlighted in 1990 by Greater Manchester Probation Service in a document entitled "HIV/AIDS Harm Reduction". Included as one of the issues to be addressed is

> *"the need to ensure that all clients have access to harm reduction, including those whose supervisor is uneasy with this Policy. This will involve ensuring that local systems are in place to ensure equality of access for clients."*

Sharps boxes and clean injecting equipment are now available in probation offices in many parts of the country, but an effective harm -reduction service needs to incorporate current knowledge about drug use. The existence of specialised posts in some services should enable new information to be collated and disseminated. Both drugs of choice and user groups vary greatly from one locality to another and patterns can change rapidly. Too many drug services are still offering services predominantly to white male opiate injectors. White people have been the major recipients of drug services since the development of many services in the 1970s and early 1980s, which were geared specifically to their needs in the face of widespread panic about an upsurge in the scale of heroin use. Many services have made strenuous efforts over the years to make themselves more accessible to women whose drug use tends to be more hidden. Reasons for this are diverse and include the risk of being regarded as an unfit mother and having children taken into Care. Lack of use of drug services by women tends to be self-perpetuating as those women who do contact services have sometimes found themselves isolated in therapeutic groups or participating in activity programmes designed to appeal to men.

Until the late-1980s assumptions were widely made that the incidence of drug use (other than cannabis) in black communities was very small. Black drug users were hesitant about approaching white dominated drug agencies and were further deterred by attitudes within their own communities which sought to deny, to the outside world at least, that any problem existed. These problems have been compounded by the difficulties many drug agencies have had in dealing with drugs other than the opiates. The prescription of methadone provides an incentive for opiate users to make and maintain contact with agencies. Crack use (and particularly the injection of crack) and other stimulants create different problems. There have always been few doctors willing or able to prescribe stimulants, and other forms of therapy offered to opiate users have been less successful for some stimulant users. Positive results are now being reported by agencies offering alternative therapies (particularly acupuncture, massage and aromatherapy) to stimulant users. The need to ascertain the scale and nature of drug use in the various ethnic minority communities has been recognised to a greater extent in the early 1990s and some drug agencies are embarking on work specifically in this area now. Probation staff need regular training to enable them to relate the principles of harm reduction to different forms of drug use, to understand the different nature of drug use and responses to it in the various communities, and to reduce the risk of drug-related harm other than HIV. Other blood-borne infections and poor injecting techniques can be particularly dangerous.

PRISON WORK

In prisons the initial response to the hysterical media attention given to HIV was to give in to the demands of untrained and frightened staff and prisoners by isolating those prisoners known to have HIV or suspected of having the virus. This was done under the Viral Infectivity Restrictions introduced in 1985 as a response to hepatitis B. Prisoners identified as being HIV positive, or suspected of belonging to a "high risk group" because they were known to be gay or to inject drugs, were held either in the prison hospital or on a separate unit. Those merely under suspicion usually remained under VIR until they agreed to an HIV test and produced a negative result. Regimes were often very limited because prisoners under VIR could not mix with other prisoners. Although the Prison Service (as it was before becoming the Prison Service Agency in 1993) always denied that the medical confidentiality of a prisoner's diagnosis was destroyed by VIR (because VIR applied to hepatitis and HIV) the effect was that prisoners on VIR were identifiable and were stigmatised. Anyone going into prison knowing that they had HIV had to make a choice between saying nothing, going on normal location and having no access to treatment or information, or telling the medical officer and being segregated under VIR. During the late-1980s the use of VIR decreased dramatically as the hysteria diminished and prison staff and prisoners understood more about

HIV. The Prison Service produced a training package for staff and prisoners, and many "outside" agencies around the country started working with prisoners and staff to improve their levels of HIV awareness and provide individual support for prisoners concerned about HIV. The VIR policy was officially abandoned in 1991 after receiving criticism in the Woolf report and a number of reports from the Prison Inspectorate. Unfortunately once confidentiality has been breached it is impossible to reprotect information. The legacy of VIR is that some long-term prisoners are still unable to mix freely with others and remain isolated.

Part of the Prison Service strategy has been the development of multi-disciplinary committees at each prison to monitor the way HIV is being dealt with and modify local policy as necessary. The prison probation team is usually represented on this committee.

Apart from offering support and information to prisoners, one of the major roles prison-based probation officers can undertake is to facilitate contact between prisoners and specialist HIV organisations. If an HIV organisation books appointments with named prisoners it becomes obvious to everyone, from the gate officer to the landing officer, that the prisoner is concerned about HIV. Probation officers have helped by enabling HIV workers to come to the prison as Voluntary Associates. Prisoners wishing to seek help can then arrange, via the probation officer, to see the Voluntary Associate without having to identify themselves to gate and landing staff as having concerns around HIV.

Anecdotal evidence suggests that some prison officers believe there is now so little concern about HIV that confidentiality is hardly an issue any more. Probation officers can help by reminding other staff that the reduction in levels of fear does not mean that an individual's right to confidentiality has diminished in any way.

TRAINING

The need for training has been mentioned several times in this chapter. It is essential that probation staff of all grades know how the transmission of HIV can be prevented so that they can adopt appropriate health and safety measures in the workplace and not harbour unreasonable fears about their risk of infection at work. Probation staff are ideally placed to provide information designed to reduce the risk of HIV transmission to people they are in contact with, who may not be in touch with other agencies and whose activities are placing them at risk. HIV also creates a greater focus on other areas such as confidentiality, child protection, drug use, sexuality, death and illness.

Information about HIV, its transmission and impact on social work practice should now be part of every social work course. In 1992 the Central Council for Education and Training in Social Work produced a publication entitled "HIV and AIDS in the Diploma in Social Work" as part of its "Improving Social Work Education and Training" series. If the outcomes suggested are being achieved, newly qualified probation officers should be joining the probation service with a good standard of knowledge about HIV and its prevention and having considered the other issues mentioned above.

However, newly qualified probation officers form a very small proportion of those employed by any probation service. The importance of providing adequate training not only to probation officers but also to unqualified staff in hostels, community service schemes and probation centres as well as clerical and cleaning staff was mentioned briefly above. If staff are not offered the chance to understand the issues and become confident with the information available about HIV, then it is unrealistic to expect them to implement the policies developed.

In 1993 a survey of all probation areas conducted by John Porter for a Health Education Authority/Standing Conference on Drug Abuse project revealed that 27 out of 55 provided little or no HIV training. In those areas providing little, individual staff members could attend courses, or specialists might be brought in to individual probation units, but it was arranged on an *ad hoc* basis and initiated by individuals. A further 15 provided some HIV training though not usually as an integrated part of a training strategy. In these areas HIV tended to be included as part of induction or first aid courses. Substantial HIV training was undertaken in only 13 areas at that time, and in some of these HIV was integrated into all courses, particularly those addressing racism and homophobia.

Some of the areas surveyed preferred to send staff on external courses rather than running training specifically for probation workers. This has the advantage of broadening the issues likely to arise and enabling staff to learn about the diversity of approaches adopted by other agencies. Others have used a "cascade" training model which involves an initial expert input, usually from an HIV trainer, to staff of all grades who are then responsible for ensuring that new staff receive HIV training as part of their induction. The disadvantage of this is that it relies upon those initially trained retaining correct information and being able to pass it on adequately. The probation staff taking on the training role in this model also need to keep up to date with new developments in the HIV field. This is difficult without access to specialist journals since news about HIV tends to become distorted and inaccurate in all sections of the general media. Another method is for a trained probation officer and an external HIV trainer to develop and run training courses together. This co-training method has the advantage of combining expert HIV knowledge with a particular insight into the specific concerns of probation staff.

Although it is possible that more probation areas are now offering HIV training as part of their training strategy, it seems that the implementation of the Criminal Justice Act 1991 and the introduction of National Standards have taken up a large amount of probation training resources over recent years. If probation staff are to stay abreast of developments in the treatment and prevention of HIV, and of the facilities available to those with the virus, then probation services need to develop rolling programmes of training incorporating initial training in HIV awareness, and updates to maintain a high standard of current knowledge. Ideally there should also be a connection between the updating of knowledge and the development of policy. HIV policies cannot be static, written once and in place for ever. There is a need for constant review and development in light of changes in medical information, the attitudes of other agencies and other local factors.

WORK WITH OTHER AGENCIES

Clients affected by HIV are likely to need long term support in relation to many aspects of their lives. Lifestyle changes, harm-reduction advice, and the need for support in relation to illness, loss, change, disability and stigma can all place heavy demands on any agency seeking to offer help. In some areas of the country there are few specialist agencies offering help and support to people with HIV, but in most towns and cities there is a range of options available. Since the need for help and support may well be long term it is often preferable for the source of that support to be an agency other than the probation service. Involvement with the probation service tends to be time limited by court orders, and the role of the probation officer has changed in such a way that the level of involvement with individual clients has decreased in recent years.

The introduction of partnership arrangements with specialist service providers has resulted in great changes in the way probation services relate to other agencies. Many services work in partnership with specialist drug agencies who may have more experience and better facilities than probation services to offer drug users with HIV.

Although partnership with HIV agencies is less likely to be an option because they are unlikely to be offering the sort of programme that partnership was designed for, referral of clients with HIV to specialist agencies may offer them the highest quality of service. Specialist HIV agencies are likely to have more experience of the difficulties facing individuals with HIV or AIDS than probation officers, and more information about the resources available to help. It is important that probation staff referring clients to other agencies are aware of the range and diversity of services on offer in their area. People with HIV cannot be considered a homogeneous group and some services are likely to be less appropriate than others for people with particular needs. People with HIV can seek assistance from those specialist agencies in the same way as any other member of the community, whereas the relationship with the probation officer is always set against a backdrop where the basis for contact is the sentence of the court, and the probation officer has the power to return the client to court in the event of non-compliance. On the other hand, where no appropriate agency exists, or where the client prefers not to deal with a specialist agency, the onus is likely to fall on the probation officer to provide what help and support is possible.

CONCLUSION

More than ten years into the British HIV epidemic it seems that on many fronts progress has been rather slow. The fact that some probation services still seem to lack policies in relation to HIV and to harm reduction is quite appalling. HIV policies which do exist vary enormously. Some are simply copies of the ACOP document on confidentiality with few modifications, suggesting that relatively little work has been done at a local level. Others are comprehensive and helpful documents designed with a review structure so that changes can be made to take account of developments in knowledge and variations in local need.

As a result of competing demands it seems that HIV training has been given a relatively low priority in some areas. It is unrealistic to expect that staff will be able to implement good practice guidance unless they understand the rationale behind it. All areas should have a training strategy in relation to HIV to ensure that all staff feel confident with their knowledge and able to operate according to local practice guidance. There is an urgent need for areas that have not yet done so to adopt harm-reduction policies. Where they already exist it is vital that they are applied consistently so that all clients are offered the same opportunities. The move towards embracing harm reduction may be the most positive outcome from all the tragedy associated with HIV, offering the opportunity to work with hard to reach drug users on terms which are negotiated rather than imposed.

References

Advisory Council on the Misuse of Drugs, *Aids and Drug Misuse Part 1*, HMSO, 1987

Advisory Council on the Misuse of Drugs, *Drug Misusers and the Criminal Justice System Part 1 Community Resources and the Probation Service*, HMSO, 1991

Association of Chief Officers of Probation, *HIV,AIDS, Confidentiality and the Probation Service*, ACOP, 1989

Bild, M. & Hayes, P. *The Problems Inherent in the Promotion of a Harm Reduction Strategy in an Agency Operating Within the Criminal Justice System*, Inner London Probation Service, 1990

Gardiner, J. D. & Talbot, J. *Northumbria Service Dependency Manual*, Northumbria Probation Service, 1990

Hindson, M. G. *HIV/AIDS Harm Reduction*, Greater Manchester Probation Service, 1990

Inner London Probation Service, *Policy Statement Drug and Alcohol Misusing Offenders*, 1993

Inner London Probation Service, *Drug and Alcohol Misusers Strategy for Action with Offenders and Alleged Offenders*, 1993

Porter, J. *HIV/AIDS Training in the Probation Service in England and Wales*, Health Education Authority/Standing Conference on Drug Abuse, 1993

Turner, C. *HIV and AIDS in the Diploma in Social Work*, Central Council for Education and Training in Social Work, 1992

NINE: WORKING WITH PEOPLE WHO HAVE COMMITED SEXUAL OFFENCES - WHAT VALUES UNDERPIN THE BEHAVIOUR AND WHAT VALUE BASE ARE WE USING IN ATTEMPTING TO ADDRESS IT?

Bryan Gocke

Firstly, acknowledgement needs to be made of the values that are likely to be implicit in anything written by a middle class, white, heterosexual male professional. Indeed this in itself runs counter to current notions of good practice in working with perpetrators which would normally advocate mixed gender pairing . However, through reasons beyond anybody's control this particular chapter was commissioned at very short notice and I felt that the only practical option was to write it on my own.

Probation officers work with individual offenders, but the values that are brought to this work by both workers and clients are obviously generated and circumscribed by social attitudes. It is therefore essential that this chapter begins with an acknowledgement of the societal context in which sexual offending, and attempts to deal with it, occur.

Without wishing to spend time considering issues of definition, I would suggest that there are two crucial elements to sexual offending - sex and power. How these interact and reinforce each other in individual instances will clearly vary along a continuum from the obtaining of sexual gratification through the abuse of power, to the exercising and maintaining of power through sexual subjugation and exploitation. Our society is hierarchical and divisive - riven by stratifications of economic class, race, gender, age, ability and sexual orientation (to name the more obvious). In such a situation the exercising of power by certain groups of people over others is endemic and indeed an integral part of the dynamics that maintain the *status quo*. The dominant ideologies that legitimate this (and provide the basis for hegemonic inclusion of a substantial number of less powerful groups - see Gramsci (1971), suggest that competition between individuals is positive in that it generates individual responsibility and motivates people to contribute to society as a whole. Individuals and groups who become or remain powerless can therefore be viewed as being responsible for their situation with no acknowledgement being made of the functional and necessary role that such disadvantage plays in maintaining the system. I would suggest that the values which underpin and are maintained by such a social system are inevitably oppressive and discriminatory, setting individuals and groups against each other in competition for power and scarce resources. It is no suprise therefore that what tends to be valued in individuals in our culture is the ability to wield power over others, whilst those on the receiving end are blamed for being weak and even wilfully incompetent.

Sexual behaviour in our society is popularly viewed as being governed by natural or biological laws, although discussion is usually obscured by coyness and embarrassment. There are rigid and narrow constraints to what is publicly acceptable, centring around heterosexual relationships in which men are expected to be dominant, powerful and aggressive, and women subordinate and even accepting of a degree of force (see Notts Probation, 1992). The last few decades have seen some progress made regarding societal acceptability of homosexual relationships, but the parliamentary debacle in 1994 surrounding the age of consent for gay men is indicative of continuing prejudice and discrimination. Racism also impacts significantly on perceptions in this area, with ideologies which have their roots in colonial expediencies still resonating today in notions of black sexuality being somehow "more animal" (Davis, 1988) and uncontrollable. This continues to feed stereotypes of the "black male rapist" and the promiscuous black woman. If we add to these the embarrassment that usually accompanies consideration of sexual practices and disability, I would invite you to conclude that as a society we lack an informed discourse regarding sex and are indeed hindered in developing one by a proliferation of pornography. The values that are visible appear repressive, defensive and divisive.

Consideration of popular conceptions about sexual offending reveals a crucial contradiction in social attitudes and understanding. On the one hand is a collective denial of the extent and prevalence of sexually aggressive and abusive acts, which incorporates a trivialisation of many victim experiences and the defining of a high threshold before behaviour is labelled abusive. On the other hand outrage is often expressed towards people who are labelled as perpetrators with terms such as "monsters", "beasts" etc. serving to mark perpetrators out as being qualitatively different from "normal", "decent" people. This contradiction permeates popular discussion, for while a consensus exists that sex with children and rape of adult women is wrong, judgements about individual instances are usually receptive to the notion that the victim may have encouraged the abuse, misunderstood the behaviour or even have fabricated it.

172

Nevertheless, despite these ambivalences, there has been what feels like a grudgingly slow acceptance in the last decade that sexual offending is a social phenomenon that requires attention and intervention and this has been accompanied, and to some extent generated, by increasing theoretical interest.

Research throughout the 1980s indicated an increasing awareness of the prevalence of sexual offending to the point where it is now being suggested that it is endemic in our society (e.g. Pringle, 1993). Estimates of rates of abuse have risen in this country from 1 in 8 girls and 1 in 12 boys in 1984 (MORI Poll) to 1 in 2 girls and 1 in 4 boys in 1991 (Kelly, 1991). Alongside this has come the reluctant acceptance of the obvious - that perpetrators are overwhelmingly male (e.g. Finkelhor, 1990).

As the evidence mounted, two strong theoretical strands, originating from different value bases, began offering explanations - Feminism and Cognitive Behavioural Psychology. Feminism quite rightly highlighted that sexual offending is a gender issue and posed the question "why?" An analysis of patriarchy supplied the answer, positing that sexual offending was part of a continuum of male behaviour that exercised collective and individual power over women and children in order that men be serviced economically, domestically and sexually. Perpetrators are not qualitatively different from "normal" men - they *are* normal men, inhabiting a common continuum of values and attitudes towards women, children and relationships (see Brownmiller, 1975). The bluff had been called! Hidden beneath the public protestations of anger towards perpetrators is what Burt (1980) called a "rape supportive culture" in which all men can be viewed as potential perpetrators , socialised as they are within patriachal values of male supremacy (see Jackson, 1982). Of course Feminism is not just a theoretical discourse but also and essentially a political movement; seeking social changes to benefit women, re-empowering victims of all types of male abuse, helping abused women and children become survivors, and placing responsibility for this state of affairs where it belongs - with men in general (both individually and collectively) and perpetrators in particular.

It was around the issue of individual responsibility that feminism, despite its social analysis, intersected with developments in the USA within Cognitive Behavioural Psychology (with a value base situated within the academic and therapeutic establishment). This approach, sceptical of the "why?" question sought to understand how individual men embarked upon and maintained sexually abusive behaviour. Emphasis was placed on sexual offending as a process in which sexual gratification obtained from masturbation using "deviant" fantasies and offending itself served to reinforce "deviant" arousal and behaviour (see Ryan *et al* 1987; Woolfe, 1984). So in effect "how" became "why", as an analogy of addiction was employed encompassing sophisticated sub systems of cognitive distortions (Salter, 1988; O'Brien, 1992).

Explanation is therefore now available at a number of levels, albeit with tensions between the two approaches (e.g. the word "deviant", which is descriptively inaccurate and has oppressive connotations, has become fudgingly replaced on flip charts by practitioners such as myself with the at least user friendly term 'NOT OK'). Feminism has uncovered the values that underpin patriarchy and sexual offending, and challenged men to change their attitudes and control their behaviour. Cognitive Behavioural Psychology offers the prospect of control and risk reduction (by intervening in cyclical patterns of behaviour) for those men whose behaviour is judged even within a patriarchal value system as being unacceptable. It is perhaps worth noting that little of the theoretical discourse generated by these two approaches seems to have impacted on the popular conceptions of sexual offending discussed above. Men presumably feel that they have too much to lose, and even if they haven't, they have much to change.

The effect on probation practice however has been marked, as attempts to fuse the two approaches have utilised multi-factor frameworks (e.g. Finkelhor, 1986) which suggest that incidents of sexual offending are not the result of one single cause. Typically, probation officers have developed programmes which seek to address the context (male attitudes, beliefs, values, thought processes , victim-perspectives) as well as the offending behaviour itself (through systematic offence deconstruction, consideration of sexual arousal patterns etc). Central to these initiatives has been the acceptance that multiple offending may well be the norm and therefore highlighting the significant potential for further offending to occur. This in turn has brought the issue of the protection of possible future victims into focus, with the apparent intractability of the sexual assault cycle suggesting that non-intervention is ethically unsupportable, unless all perpetrators are incarcerated for ever.

The increasing insight into the process of offending, and in particular the role that cognitive distortions play in allowing perpetrators to disregard the veneer of social and legal prohibition against sexually offending, highlighted the block to effective intervention that is denial. It soon became apparent that all our new insights about the nature and extent of offending were being angrily rebuffed

174

by our clients as they sought to defend themselves against the negative consequences of full disclosure. Sex offender denial is a complex matter (Gocke, 1991), but resistance to a full acknowledgement of responsibility is understandable against internalised popular conceptions of perpetrators as "beasts". This situation has resulted in practitioners positing assumptive stances (Eldridge; 1990; Fisher and Howard, 1994) with an underlying belief that perpetrators are unlikely to be able to provide a completely honest account of their behaviour without significant external intervention. As Notts Probation (1992) point out, such a stance "fundmentally challenges a traditional social work position; namely that we believe and respect our clients' understanding of his or her experience" (18).

Along side this came other tensions and dilemmas. The concern to protect others has opened up a debate as to whether "treatment" (a term which is itself burdened in this situation by medical values) should be voluntary or compulsory. It became apparent that treatment , if it was to be in any way effective, would have to be personally intrusive and challenging. Many perpetrators, wishing to maintain their cognitive distortions intact, opt not to enter treatment, while many others drop out once the going gets tough and the negative experiences of being processed through the criminal justice system have receded. In response to this many programmes have become mandated by court order. In support of such developments Salter (1988) suggests that this is the only way to provide the community with some measure of protection and risk reduction. Clarke *et al* (1990) argue that sanctions actually provide space for perpetrators to develop a genuine motivation for the work which we would be naïve to assume exists in the first place. Nevertheless, counter-arguments exist advocating that only voluntary involvement should be pursued on the grounds that coercion is unlikely to foster genuine change, and challenging the ethics of responding to abusive behaviour through punishment dressed up as treatment (Notts Probation, 1992).

This debate raises the question of "who exactly is the client in this situation?" I, along with many probation officers, find myself helping to justify the use of confrontational methods by recasting my client to be a past and potential future victim rather than the perpetrator in front of me. Ryan and Lane (1991) in commenting on this, suggest that all work in the area of sexual abuse must be seen primarily in terms of protection of the public (and in particular of children). In many ways this shifts the value base of the work towards that of a victim perspective - but leaves work with perpetrators open to abusive practices such as the "legitimised nonce bashing" described by Sheath (1990, 159-62). Indeed, as probation officers seek to maintain the all-important balance between challenge and affirmation, effective work with perpetrators will by necessity operate on terrain that is close to becoming oppressive if it is to avoid collusion. In realising this, many practitioners have modified their style to ensure that direct confrontation is used sparingly and appropriately (although the opportunity to consider issues of "timing" when preparing a PSR is in my experience limited). I am aware that I have shifted to methods that encourage perpetrators to disclose their perceptions with little comment from myself until they have generated sufficient contradictions for me to suggest that the whole thing "simply doesn't add up". I may have become less overtly confrontational and as a result increased the chances of developing a productive working relationship - but my style is undeniably more manipulative!

What seems clear is that the issue of power in the worker/client relationship is of paramount importance. As workers attempting to intervene in behaviour which appears so intractable, and faced with relentless denial, I think we often experience feelings of powerlessness - and with considerable justification. However, given the nature of the work, we exercise power that is in many ways quite alien to more traditional social work values. We offer only limited confidentiality, stating the need to protect others as the primary consideration and insist that our professional agenda be followed in an attempt to circumvent the attempts by perpetrators to divert and deflect. The result of all this, I would suggest, is that work with perpetrators typically takes place in an atmosphere of considerable tension with varying degrees of hostility and distrust in evidence. The potential for oppressive practice, and even abuse on the one hand and collusion or worker victimisation on the other, is clear. This requires that workers are aware of their own personal agendas and the impact that they may have, and that management of the work needs to be informed and rigorous.

How do we, as workers, deal with such upsetting material and the danger of "the impact of the work paralleling the impact of the abuse itself" (Ryan and Lane, 1991, 411)? Coping strategies will clearly differ according to the individual, their life experiences (Ryan, 1988 suggests that 45 per cent of workers have been victims themselves) and, I suspect, crucially their gender. My experience as a trainer when working with single gender groups, is that women find it far easier to discuss their feelings in relation to this work than men, who often seem disempowered by the guilt of association. Women feel anger and frustration at the situation and easily make links with their own victim experiences in general, coping daily as they do within a patriarchal society. The values common in the wider society of course make them more vulnerable to oppressive gender dynamics when working with perpetrators, and indeed male colleagues.

For men there is considerable discomfort with having to take on board the actions of our own sex, and responses to the anger and hostility directed at men in general vary from glum acknowledgement to defensive denial. How this is translated into work with clients is of course crucial, with MacLeod and Sarager (1991) asking "if it is our business to prove that we are not abusers" and is the work "our vehicle for the expression of violent feelings by proxy" (43)? As a male worker, having entered the field partly in response to feminist assertions that sexual abuse was a male problem, I think I deal with the tensions between the personal/professional/political largely through dissonance. For periods of time I operate apparently untouched by the horror and despair of the details of the offending and how it relates to my own male attitudes and values, concentrating instead on the process of intervention. However, at fairly regular intervals this is pierced by an issue or an instance which brings out the sheer awfulness of the situation, leaving me upset, angry, depressed and self-doubting. At such times, thinking about values and motivations can be extremely painful - but in my view essential if my practice is to remain acceptable and if I am to change as a man.

In more general terms, our theoretical progress leaves probation officers facing a particular set of problems. Expectations of denial, minimisations and rationalisations result in us assuming far more and worse behaviours than our clients are likely to admit, at least in the first instance. This can have the rather strange effect of us only feeling satisfied by disclosure of the worst. Many of us will have felt huge relief when a perpetrator finally acknowledges something crucial to his offending that we'd expected all along (and may well have told him so before only to have met angry denial). The relief is due to us not having misread the situation and feeling that it had been justifiable to resist attempts by him to groom us into collusion with his denials - but it is an uncomfortable feeling to set alongside the uncovering of behaviour which would have been particularly traumatic for the victim!

Other difficulties result from the "lack of closure" that the work affords (Ryan and Lane, 1991: 412). Given our understanding of the potential for sexually aggressive behaviour to be a life-long problem, there is even less chance of an acceptable end product than there is in social work in general. There are just degrees of risk and worries that we've missed something of vital importance.

In response to this mounting list of tensions, difficulties and dilemmas, management in all agencies has often been hampered by the fact that development of the work has been largely practitioner led. Problems have arisen as it has sought to catch up, control and manage. In the Probation Service a critical thematic inspection by the Home Office in 1991 has resulted in areas producing policies and guidelines and providing much-needed training. Despite this undoubted progress, my concern would be that much of this constitutes impression management, with agency denial and minimisation of the scale and nature of the task obscuring debate about the chronic under-resourcing of this area of work. In many instances the increased insight into the risks posed by perpetrators and increased expectations of our ability to assess, intervene and manage, appear to have resulted in a burden of increasing responsibility falling overwhelmingly on individual workers. Despite a clear recognition by practitioners that mixed gender co-working represents the basis for intervention which is safe and effective, much of the work is still undertaken by probation officers working on their own. Such situations compound the pressures outlined above and increase markedly the risk of drift into oppressive or collusive practice. Supervision, where these issues should be regularly addressed, is problematic in that supervisors often have far less experience in the work than practitioners and the proceedings are often dominated by bureaucratic checking and form filling.

In this climate I think it is important to question how the work, and the probation officers undertaking it, are valued by management. For many workers the almost inevitable "burn out" is dealt with through mobility policies. There is a failure here to recognise that it takes a considerable amount of time to become competent in this area of work and that potential victims are not best served by the regular loss of experienced workers. Ryan and Lane (1991) dispute that burnout is inevitable and suggest that it should be managed through tackling the issues and the problems. Whilst the work is obviously demanding in itself, this has been exacerbated by changes in the value base within probation management. Nellis (1995) describes a shift towards a "regulatory culture . . . which imprisons practitioners . . . in a hierarchy of policies, guidelines and monitoring arrangements". I feel this serves work in this area poorly, focusing as it does on a quantitative rather than qualitative approach.

Of course management's role is not just about support - accountability in this area of work is of vital importance, including staff selection and monitoring. There have been sufficient recorded instances of sexual abuse by workers in the welfare system for all agencies to assume that it can, does, and will occur. The obvious way forward is to design procedures that will reduce the risk of such instances, but while it is painfully obvious in retrospect to see mistakes made and patterns developing, prevention seems particularly difficult. Pringle (1993) would argue that this is hardly suprising given the endemic nature of abuse in our society and, to return to the gender issue, how difficult it is to distinguish abusing from non-abusing men. He suggests that if we are serious in attempting to reduce the instances of abuse by workers then we need to consider restricting the role that male workers might have in social work, particularly with regard to victims (known or otherwise).

However, the difficulties are not confined solely to intra-agency matters. In assessing and working with sex offenders, the probation service is located within the criminal justice system, which in turn brings further contradictions and of course dilemmas and conflicts about underlying values. The legal framework in which sexual offending is dealt with embodies and mediates some of the core values of our society, seeking as it does to maintain the *status quo* of public morality. As this is essentially patriarchal, racist, heterosexist and class based, we should expect to find further manifestations of the oppression and discrimination inherent in the system. Gay men remain discriminated against in terms of age of consent and have restrictions placed on the expression of their sexuality. Black offenders in general are dealt with more harshly when sentenced and less likely to be offered treatment (see Notts Probation, 1992). On top of this, the criminal justice system is essentially ageist, with the veracity of children's evidence easily challenged under the current rules of evidence - and subverted by adults in court. This is despite strong indications that fabrication of evidence by young victims is likely to be rare (see Salter, 1988). The effect of this is to favour perpetrators (men) against victims (women and children) as conviction is often difficult to obtain without a confession and with the result that the Crown Prosecution Service is particularly cautious about prosecuting.

The Probation Service has developed clear anti-discriminatory and anti oppressive policy statements and the last few years have witnessed considerable efforts to implement them in practice. However, in the field of sexual offending the provision for perpetrators appears to be targeted at guess who? - white, heterosexual men! Group work in particular (which is rightly viewed as a powerful vehicle for the work) is inherently oppressive of minority groups of people. Black perpetrators are rarely referred to groups because of (mainly white) workers' concern for their well-being in a predominantly white atmosphere, and often no appropriate alternatives are offered. Gay men are more often included - but typically little attention is given to how they can be helped to deal with the homophobic comments they are likely to meet. As for women perpetrators, the provision is almost non-existent, with the understandable confusion about the gender dynamic provoking uncertainty as to how best to proceed. A key issue yet to be adequately addressed is the viability of using frameworks and interventions developed for male abusers in work with female offenders.

But before a perpetrator can enter the "treatment system" probation officers have to engage in and attempt to influence the court process itself. Here is an immediate clash of values as the system penalises honesty, one of the crucial goals of intervention, through harsher sentencing . In conjunction with this, the common activity of plea bargaining (linked to the difficulties of conviction) often results in powerful reinforcement of perpetrator denial with particularly negative repercussions in later treatment (see Gocke, 1991).

For probation officers, the central issue in assessment at this stage is the consideration of disposal options. Given our knowledge of the intractability of sexually aggressive behaviour and our rightful concern to reduce the number of future victims, continued adherence to the value of anti-custodialism must be debated. Despite the fact that imprisonment is essentially about punishment, it does provide a limited protection to the public which may well be the best on offer. I am thinking particularly about cases where the behaviour is so appalling or persistent (and often both) that community sentences would provide little in the way of future public protection. I also remain mystified as to the best course of action in a situation where someone has been found guilty but maintains his innocence through report stage. Given the difficulties of the work even with an acknowledgement of guilt, can a proposal favouring a community sentence on the grounds of anti-custodialism be anything but collusive in this instance?

Of course the debate will be informed by our knowledge that the prison system tends to decrease perpetrators' ability to take responsibility for past and future behaviour - largely due to their own victimisation and oppression whilst incarcerated (see Gocke, 1991). Even the recent introduction of the "core programme" of treatment only caters for prisoners serving in excess of four years, and crucially still takes place within a larger jail culture of extreme sexism and violence. As such, prison as a place where the risk of sexually reoffending might be managed and reduced must be severely questioned (see Cowburn, 1991). Indeed, since the introduction of the Criminal Justice Act 1991, practitioner concerns around sentencing have focused on the imprisonment of perpetrators for short and medium terms where some degree of guilt has been admitted and where PSRs have made strong cases for treatment and monitoring packages within the community. Incarceration in these instances would appear to combine the worst of all worlds - the negative entrenchment of attitudes and values within prison, with public protection provided only in the immediate period. Nevertheless, sentencing has an undeniable social impact, with Kelly *et al* (1992) pointing out that a reduction in custodial sentencing for sex offenders would contribute a significant social statement regarding the severity with which sexual offending is viewed.

Probation Service involvement in the child protection system provides a further context for examining our value base. Again, the concern to try and protect others suggests that "rehabilitation alone is insufficient as a value base for probation . . . because the placing of offenders' needs and interests above, as opposed to alongside, the rights of victims and the requirements of public safety lacks moral justification and, in the 1990s political credibility" (Nellis, 1995).

But even without probation dilemmas, the child protection system has problems of its own, with social workers blamed if they act and blamed if they don't - a direct reflection through the media of societal ambivalence. Social workers, and increasingly probation officers, are expected to undertake risk assessments on which perpetrators' future contact with children will rest, with a certainty that all our theoretical and practice experience tells us cannot exist. We are again in the realms of relative risk-taking against a backdrop where the balance of power has tilted significantly towards parents (and hence perpetrators) in recent years. The Children Act 1989 tells us to listen to what children say they want to happen, on the face of it a perfectly reasonable and potentially empowering stance. However, this is so difficult to operate when we know that a victim (and for that matter siblings and non-abusing partners) are likely to be influenced in their views by the perpetrators' long term grooming both during offending and following arrest. As Salter (1992) pointed out, just because the offending has stopped it doesn't necessarily mean that the abuse has ceased. In considering child protection issues we must be careful "not to talk to the perpetrator inside the victim's head" and "when a child victim states that she wants her father back, she may well mean that she wants him back and for the abuse never to have happened" (Fairfield, 1993).

Public and official expectations of the child protection system indicate a naïvety about the nature and extent of the problem of sexual abuse and our ability to deal effectively with it on a piecemeal basis. Public enquiries such as Cleveland, whilst making no attempt to address why men sexually abuse and blaming the influence of feminism for over-reaction by workers, make an assumption that our systems are capable, if implemented correctly by social workers and probation officers, of adequately protecting children from sexual abuse (see MacLeod and Sarager, 1991). They go on to question this assumption, suggesting that the reality is in stark contrast - "we simply do not know how to prevent abuse" (30).

This raises for me a critical factor in considering (if indirectly) the health of our value base in this area of work - its efficacy. If we can feel that our interventions are, on balance, having a positive effect on the situation then we may be inclined towards some cautious optimism. Unfortunately attempts to monitor effectiveness are in their infancy, with analysis complicated by the length of time required for accurate study. What I think is apparent is that the initial optimism of the mid-1980s, that use of a cognitive behavioural framework could assist perpetrators to change their attitudes and behavioural patterns, has been replaced by a realism that *control and monitoring* may be the key components of any packages offering viable public protection (Salter, 1992). Once more this sits uneasily with a more generalised social work value of the belief in the capacity of people to change. The intractability of the behaviour would suggest that change is difficult and likely to be slow, which puts into perspective the debate touched on earlier about whether treatment should be voluntary or mandatory. For me, the crucial change that I am seeking in perpetrators embodies an acceptance of the difficulties of change, of the consequences of this for the management of future risk and the need to co-operate with external controls. Expectations and hopes have altered, with success often now reframed as a reduction in the number of future victims of individual perpetrators.

The difficulties involved in work with perpetrators appear, at least in part, to be linked with the need to engage with both victim and offender perspectives in a way which is neither abusive nor collusive. This creates numerous dilemmas in a probation service that has largely viewed offenders in general as being at least partly the victim of their circumstances - which I would suggest is based on an implicit class analysis that cites poverty, unemployment, poor housing, lack of prospects, etc in mitigation. This is not an option in intervening in sexual offending, with a feminist analysis of gender relations and our understanding of the role of cognitive distortions making it imperative that sex offenders are not allowed to deflect responsibility for their actions.

In consequence, my own response to each of the core values for probation practice suggested in the introductory chapter of this book has been "yes but!" Other formulations, such as that provided by BASW, feel largely unhelpful in any attempt to understand the specific complexity of the ethical issues involved in work with perpetrators. However, I feel that a short list of core values could, and should, be stated e.g:

- Sexual offending is wrong because it harms victims.
- Victims, both past and future, should be protected.
- Perpetrators should be held responsible for their actions and future behaviour.

Having just stressed the complexity of the issues, such a short and seemingly obvious set of points might be viewed with derision (and a far more comprehensive value base which pays particular attention to anti-oppressive issues has been produced by Notts Probation (1992), but there is a lack of anything approaching a genuine societal consensus over even these basic principles). This is in turn reflected by the ambivalence in which the work is viewed by welfare agencies. In the current climate of cuts in funding, the resource-intensive implications of providing an adequate service in the area of sexual offending which properly values women, children and victims are often minimised and even ignored. It is particularly disappointing that the Probation Service has made little attempt to generate public and political debate about these concerns and in consequence serves by default to uphold the *status quo* of gender dynamics in our society - supporting men at the expense of women and children, perpetrators at the expense of victims.

In this grave situation, it is my view that practitioners and managers need to consider the values that will be necessary to develop the work so that it can play an increasing part in attempts to reduce the prevalence of sexual offending in our society. Central to this must be a commitment to avoid such work being used to legitimate patriarchal attitudes that firstly deny the scale of the problem and which, secondly, fail to acknowledge that current levels of intervention are inadequate for the task. Such a value base should include "honesty" about our limitations, the reasons for them and the need to break out of reactive isolation and engage with other social systems (such as education, child care, etc) in more preventive initiatives. Despite the pressures on us to make judgements and manage risk, "openness" to other possible types of intervention and different insights is essential if we are to avoid being drawn in our desperation into rigid orthodoxies. Finally, if agencies and individual workers (and particularly men) are to develop structures and practice that are anti-oppressive and effective we must avoid remaining defensive and actively explore our own ambivalences regarding this area of work.

References

Brownmiller, S. *Against our will*, Penguin, 1985

Burt, M. "Cultural myths and supports for rape" in *Journal of Personality and Social Psychology*, 38.2, 1980

Clark, P., Erooga, M. & Bently, M. "Protection, control and treatment: group work with child sexual abuse perpetrators" in *Groupwork* 3(2), 1980; 172 - 90

Cowburn, M. *Sex offenders in prison*, thesis submitted to the University of Nottingham for the degree of M. Phil. 1991

Davis, A. *Women, race and class*, Womens Press, 1988

Eldridge, H. "Assumptions in working with sex offenders" Gracewell Institute, 1990

Fairfield, J. Paper given at NOTA national conference , University of Warwick, 1993

Finkelhor, D. "Sexual abuse in a national survey of adult men and women : Prevalence , characteristics and risk factors" in *Child Abuse and Neglect* 14, 1990; 19-28.

Finkelhor, D. *A source book on child sexual abuse*, Sage, 1986

Fisher, D. & Howard, P. Workshop at NOTA national conference , University of Durham, 1994

Gocke, B. *Tackling denial in sex offenders*, UEA, Social Work Monograph, Norwich, 1991

Gramsci, A. *Selections from the prison notebooks,* Lawrence and Wishart, 1971

Jackson, S. *Childhood and Sexuality,* Blackwell, Oxford, 1982

Kelly, L. *et al* "And what happened to him? Policy on sex offenders from the survivor's perspective" in *Beyond containment : the penal response to sex offending,* Prison Reform Trust, 1992

Kelly, L. *et al, An exploratory study of the prevalence of sexual abuse in a sample of 16 - 21 year olds,* Polytechnic of North London, 1991

MacCleod, M. & Saraga, E. "Clearing a path through the under-growth : a feminist reading of recent literature on child sexual abuse" in *Social Work and Social Welfare Year Book 3* (eds) Carter, P, Jeffs, T. & Smith, M.K. Open University Press, 1991

Nellis, M. "Towards a new view of probation values" in Hugman, R. & Smith, D. *Ethics in Social Work,* Routledge, 1995 - forthcoming

Nottinghamshire Probation Service, *Changing men : a practice guide to working with adult male sex offenders,* Notts P S, 1992

O'Brien, M. Paper given at NOTA national conference , University of Dundee, 1992

Pringle, K. "Child sexual abuse perpetrated by welfare personnel and the problem of men" in *Critical Social Policy* 36, 1993

Ryan, G., Lane, S., Davis, J. & Issacs, C. "Juvenile Sex Offenders : development and correction" in *Child Abuse & Neglect* 11, 1987; 385 - 395.

Ryan, G. and Lane, S. "The impact of sexual abuse on the interven-tionist" in *Juvenile sexual offending : causes , consequences and corrections,* Lexington, 1992

Ryan, G., Krugman, R. & Miyoshi, T. Results of the early childhood experience survey presented at the 17th National Symposium on Child Abuse and Neglect , Keystone , Colorado, 1988

Salter, A. Paper given at NOTA national conference , University of Dundee, 1992

Salter, A. *Treating child sex offenders and victims,* Sage, 1988

Sheath, M. "Confrontative work with sex offenders : legitimised nonce bashing?" in *Probation Journal*, December, 1990

Woolfe, S. *Evaluation and treatment of the sex offender*, Sexual Assault Centre Publications, Seattle, 1984